BIBLE SEEDS
FOR ENRICHING YOUR
—→ CHARACTER ←—

STARBURST PUBLISHERS

P.O. Box 4123 Lancaster, PA 17604

CREDITS:
Cover design by Richmond & Williams
Text design and composition by Booksetters

Unless otherwise indicated all Scripture was taken from the HOLY BIBLE:
NEW INTERNATIONAL VERSION® NIV®. Copyright © 1973, 1978, 1984
by International Bible Society.

Bible Seeds for Enriching Your Character:
A Simple Study-Devotional for Growing in God's Word
Copyright © 2002 Starburst, Inc.
Starburst Publishers, P.O. Box 4123, Lancaster, PA 17604
All rights reserved.

ISBN: 0-7394-3048-3
Printed in USA

Introduction

Every piece of refreshing, mouthwatering fruit began as a tiny seed. With good soil, proper nutrients, and enough sunshine, the seeds burst through the ground, grew into trees, and blossomed into nourishing fruit.

In a similar way God's Word is filled with small seeds, or verses, waiting to blossom in the fertile soil of a woman's heart. The more we learn of God's Word the more we become like Christ and gain the ability to nurture those around us in a godly way. Maturity of character begins by developing such fruit as love, joy, and peace.

In about five minutes you can feed and water the fruit of your spirit with each three-page lesson. Don't worry if you don't know much about the Bible. The creators of the *God's Word for the Biblically-Inept™* series had you in mind when they developed this book. All women, from beginners to mature women of faith, can find sustenance in these pages.

Begin by reading the Bible verse or "seed" and the lesson about that seed. For tasty morsels of insight from the original languages of the Bible, don't miss the "Dig Deeper" word study at the bottom of the first page.

The "Background Bulb" brings additional biblical or

historical information to help you better understand the day's seed. The "Weed and Water" feature highlights how you can apply the lesson to your life. The "Sprout and Scatter" feature details ways you can nurture others as you practice the biblical principles that are discussed.

To help you put your new insights into practice, grab a pen or pencil and answer the "Think about it" questions. Then write your own ending for the "Prayer Pot." Finish each lesson by reading the takeaway beside the fruit. Studying God's Word is fast and easy.

Bible Seeds for Enriching Your Character will help you grow in qualities of love, joy, peace, patience, kindness, goodness, faithfulness, gentleness, and self-control. You'll be harvesting the fruit of a godly character before you know it!

—Starburst Editors

Fruit of the Spirit

Today's Seed

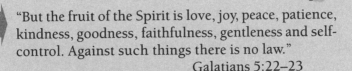

"But the fruit of the Spirit is love, joy, peace, patience, kindness, goodness, faithfulness, gentleness and self-control. Against such things there is no law."

Galatians 5:22–23

Stop by any roadside fruit stand during the summer and your senses become overloaded with sights and smells of colorful, juicy, fresh fruit. You can't wait to touch and taste it. Makes you want at least one of every kind!

Paul described life in the Spirit as filled with fruit—not bananas, strawberries, and watermelon—but love, joy, peace, patience, goodness, kindness, faithfulness, gentleness, and self-control.

Christians have been admitted into God's spiritual orchard. Our ticket is Jesus Christ. Jesus has done what no one who ever lived could do—he lived a perfect life and died to pay the penalty for our sins. Then he conquered death by rising again. Now Christ intercedes for us before God, and he puts on his spiritual gardening gloves to transform us to be like him in godly character.

When we met Jesus and accepted his offer of salvation, he planted us securely in the soil of salvation. He grafted limbs of

Dig Deeper:

The word "Spirit" comes from the Greek word *pneuma,* meaning the third person of the Trinity—the Holy Spirit. As Christians we no longer produce fruit of our own spirits, but now the Holy Spirit produces new fruit in us.

spiritual fruit-bearing trees to our "trunk." Our tree is no longer what it used to be. Love replaces envy. Joy defeats disappointment. Peace reigns over chaos. Kindness, goodness, and gentleness replace selfishness, harshness, and intolerance. Faithfulness grows roots in place of infidelity, and self-control overcomes extremes in appetites and attitudes. Makes you want to produce one of every kind!

Background Bulb:

In the verses that precede today's seed, Paul wrote, "It is for freedom that Christ has set us free" (Galatians 5:1). We are delivered from the wrath of God and the power of sin. Legalism's rules have lost control over us. Some think this freedom allows us to live as we please—grabbing all the money, power, sex, and pleasure we can. But true Christian freedom means we delight in the power of the Holy Spirit and the fruit he develops in us.

Weed and Water:

When left to ourselves we produce blemished fruit—envy, discord, flightiness, rebellion, and unkindness. To develop godly fruit we must be living by the Spirit, allowing God to stretch us in areas we've never ventured before—generosity, trust, humility, and compassion. The fruit of the Spirit grows on our branches when we stay attached to Jesus, the vine, through prayer and meditation in his Word.

Think about it:

List some ways that you see the Spirit's fruit ripening in your life.

- _____
- _____
- _____
- _____

What will you do to allow God to stretch you further toward developing the fruit of the Spirit?

_____
_____
_____

Prayer Pot:

Lord, help me become a fruit-bearing Christian by . . .

_____
_____
_____
_____
_____

God wants spiritual fruit, not religious nuts.

Love on Display

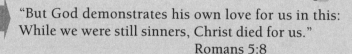

Today's
Seed

"But God demonstrates his own love for us in this:
While we were still sinners, Christ died for us."
Romans 5:8

There is a nationally syndicated cartoon entitled "Love Is . . .".
This one-panel comic gives a single-line definition of love
beneath the drawing. The accompanying text says such things as:
"Love is putting a happy note in his lunch box;" "Love is remembering her birthday;" "Love is saying, 'I'm sorry.'"

If today's seed were a "Love Is . . ." panel, the picture would
show Christ dying on the cross in pain and agony. Little charac-
ters at the foot of the cross would be involved in many kinds of
sin, including hammering nails into Christ's feet, spitting on him,
and laughing at him. The caption would read, "Love is Christ
dying for you while you still hated him."

The God kind of love pours out on us because that's what God
determined he would do. We did nothing to earn his love. Just as
rain falls on the grass and the weeds alike, so God's love is available to all—the preacher and the prostitute alike.

Dig Deeper:

The word "demonstrates" comes from a Greek word
meaning "to exhibit." God put his love for us on open display when Jesus died for us.

Background Bulb:

Jesus knew exactly why he had come to earth. He was a man on an incredible mission. Before his birth, the angel told his parents that their son would save his people from their sins. He told his disciples he had come to be an example to the world of what God the Father was like. He told a crowd that if they destroyed him, he would rise in three days. Jesus knew that in his death he would exhibit God's love to mankind.

Sprout and Scatter:

As God has shown his love for us, it is incumbent upon us to show his love to others. Jesus once told his disciples, "I have set you an example that you should do as I have done for you" (John 13:15). He said this after washing his disciples' feet, an act of love and service. Jesus' actions throughout his life can give us ideas of how to express God's love to those around us. Jesus fed the hungry, encouraged the downhearted, touched the hurting, and told everyone he met about his Father. When we do these things for others, we show them God's love. (See Matthew 25:34–40.)

Think about it:

What guilt are you holding onto about your past sin?

_____

Write today's seed, replacing the phrase "while we were yet sinners" with "while I was still (your sin)."

_____

_____

Now that you have experienced God's love, how can you reach out, showing that love to someone else today?

_____

_____

Prayer Pot:

Father, I adore you. Help me to lay my life before you by . . .

_____

_____

_____

_____

_____

"Amazing love! how can it be That
Thou, my God, shouldst die for me!"
—Charles Wesley

Wow!

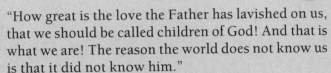

Today's Seed ▶ "How great is the love the Father has lavished on us, that we should be called children of God! And that is what we are! The reason the world does not know us is that it did not know him."

1 John 3:1

The youngest of a father's two sons decides he must have his share of the family inheritance—now! The father obliges and the son moves away with his newly acquired fortune, thinking he's about to have the time of his life. But before long his wild lifestyle has stolen every cent of the inheritance, and the son realizes he is worse off than his father's employees back home. In need of food and shelter but feeling unworthy of his father's love, he decides to go home, admit his wrong, and beg his father to take him in as a hired hand. (See Luke 15:11–32.)

As the son trudges home, practicing his please-take-me-back speech, he comes in sight of his father's property. He sees a man running toward him and figures it's some servant doing a rush job. As the figure gets closer, the son realizes it's his father—rushing toward

Dig Deeper:
Love gives. The word "lavished" used in today's seed is the same word translated "gave" in John 3:16: "For God so loved the world that He gave his one and only Son. . . ."

him with arms outstretched. Before the son knows what's happening, he is wrapped in a bear hug.

"I-I'm sorry—" the son stammers.

"Forget about it!" the father cries as he wipes tears of joy from his face. "Quick, bring the best clothes and shoes," the father hollers to his servants. "Give him my ring. It's time to party!"

The father isn't angry. He doesn't say, "I told you so." He doesn't even say, "Next time what do you think you could do differently?" He just envelops the young man in his great love.

Wow!

Background Bulb:

John, the author of today's seed, called himself "the disciple whom Jesus loved" (John 21:20). John was one of Jesus' closest friends and was present on special occasions: at Jesus' transfiguration (Matthew 17) and the Garden of Gethsemane (Mark 14). It was into John's care that Jesus left his own mother when he was dying on the cross. John was also a witness of the resurrected Lord and a recipient of the Holy Spirit on the day of Pentecost. Yes, John knew of lavished love.

Weed and Water:

We all feel inadequate sometimes. The next time you doubt yourself, remember the love God has lavished on you. Tell yourself some true things: "God adopted me into his family," "I am a child of God," and "God knows all about me but loves me anyway." Look at all God has given you. Then move on to things like: "I'm an honest person," or "I'm a good friend."

Think about it:

How does knowing about God's lavished love make you feel about yourself?

_____

_____

_____

Who do you know that could benefit from hearing about God's incredible love?

_____

_____

_____

Prayer Pot:

Dear God, thank you for making me part of your family. Help me experience your love when . . .

_____

_____

_____

_____

_____

"How priceless is your unfailing love!
Both high and low among men find
refuge in the shadow of your wings."
—Psalm 36:7

Hang in There

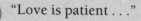

Today's Seed

> "Love is patient . . ."
>
> 1 Corinthians 13:4a

You may have heard the saying, "She has the patience of Job." It is usually said of someone who doesn't blow up when provoked, lose their temper when wrongly confronted, or lash out when harshly treated. These people confound us. Someone with the patience of Job seems to be able to be pushed and pushed, yet she rarely pushes back. *How can she stand that kind of treatment?* we wonder. *She must be seething on the inside, but she looks so calm. If that happened to me I'd . . .*

The woman who exhibits such remarkable patience has probably developed this virtue over time, and she has discovered that patience is an effect of having love for others.

Love and concern for your fellow human beings calms you down. You are able to look past a gruff exterior or a sharp word to the heart of the person before you. You readily recognize when the poor treatment you are receiving is not your fault, but rather a result of the person's own problems.

Dig Deeper:

The Greek word for "patience" can also be translated "long-spirited" or "long-suffering." It carries the idea of enduring with people and their needs.

Love helps you empathize, putting yourself in the other woman's pumps and feeling her stress. Love also realizes that it may take longer than the next minute, hour, day, week, month, or year before you no longer have to deal with that person. But all of that is OK because that's one key aspect of love—it hangs in there. Love is patient.

Background Bulb:

The Book of Job is about a man who had a myriad of troubles. In one day, he lost everything that was dear to him except his wife. And rather than encouraging him while he was in despair, she told him to "curse God and die!" (Job 2:9). Still, Job maintained his faith in God and patiently waited for God's resolution to his problems. In this same story we can also see patience exhibited by God toward Job as God patiently allowed Job to seek answers during his struggles.

Weed and Water:

The next time you find your patience with someone running thin, try putting yourself in the other person's shoes. Take a deep breath—not an audible sigh—and focus on what might be lying beneath the surface of the situation. Think about how the other person is feeling, what she (or he) may have recently been through, and why she's feeling and reacting the way she is. Actively try to understand her, putting your own feelings and wants aside.

Think about it:

What causes you to be impatient with people?

_____

_____

What can you do to show patience to the people who really work on your nerves?

_____

_____

Now that you know showing patience is a way of showing love, how do you feel?

_____

_____

Prayer Pot:

Lord, please help me to exhibit love through patience the next time . . .

_____

_____

_____

_____

_____

"A patient man has great understanding, but a quick-tempered man displays folly."
—Proverbs 14:29

Love and Intimacy

Today's Seed

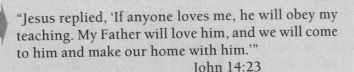

"Jesus replied, 'If anyone loves me, he will obey my teaching. My Father will love him, and we will come to him and make our home with him.'"

John 14:23

In many families, small children love to sit in their parents' laps. The child feels secure. The parent can hug, rock, and cuddle the child. The parent and child communicate with each other in soft, tender voices. They look into each other's eyes. There's nothing quite like being this close.

As children grow they learn that when they disobey their parents, they disrupt that feeling of intimacy. If they want to restore the precious sense of closeness they once shared, they have to repent and obey their parents. The more they obey, the more everyone enjoys the relationship.

Relationships, by definition, have two participants. In situations like the one mentioned above, loving parents choose to forgive the child and rebuild the intimacy. However, humans sometimes abandon or abuse child-parent relationships, unlike

Dig Deeper:

"Love" in this verse is *agapao* in Greek, meaning to love as an act of one's will and to find joy in something. When we choose to love God, he finds joy in our choice.

God. He never drops his side of the relationship. When we fail him, he's always ready to restore our intimacy with him.

Today's seed emphasizes how we increase our intimacy with God. God loves us unconditionally, never forcing his love upon us. He does, however, have standards we must obey. We love him by keeping his words. It's not that this is a performance standard; it's simply a statement of fact. As both sides do their part, intimacy grows. As we love and obey God, we become more and more aware of his abiding presence in our lives.

Weed and Water:

Spending time with and communicating with someone leads to closeness and intimacy. Beware of developing closeness with someone you shouldn't—for example, a colleague of the opposite sex. For the next week, concentrate on your communication with God. Talk to him in prayer about absolutely everything and obey him in every way you can. At the end of the week, gauge the level of intimacy you feel with God.

Sprout and Scatter:

Make it a project to demonstrate your love to your loved ones. Call friends you haven't talked to in some time. Give a hug. Sit with your kids as they watch a television show that they like (and don't make any negative comments or facial expressions). Find a new way to show your intimate feeling toward your spouse.

Think about it:

With whom do you feel a special closeness? Why?

_____

_____

_____

_____

Does your style of communication invite intimacy? If so, how? If not, why not?

_____

_____

_____

Prayer Pot:

Lord, help me to be more intimate with you when . . .

_____

_____

_____

_____

_____

_____

Intimacy with God thrives on communication.

Just Be Nice

Today's Seed

"Love is kind."

1 Corinthians 13:4b

The religious leaders had heard Jesus teach, and what he said really rubbed them the wrong way. He had a tremendous following—of the people who should have been following them. The leaders were out to get him, to trip him up. (See John 8:4–11.)

As Jesus was teaching one morning, the leaders burst in and thrust a woman into the midst of the group. "Teacher," they said, "this woman has been caught in the act of adultery. In the law Moses commanded us to stone such women. What now do you say?" (John 8:5).

Jesus appeared to be in a tough spot. If he agreed to punish the woman, all his talk of compassion would go out the window and he'd lose credibility with the crowd. If he pardoned her outright, however, he'd clearly go against the law of Moses and his credibility as a rabbi would be shot. They had him.

Caught off guard? Not Jesus. He simply said, "If any one of you is without sin, let him be the first to throw a stone at her" (John 8:7). One by one the woman's accusers walked away. Jesus did not

Dig Deeper:
To be kind means to show oneself useful. A kind act is a benevolent act.

allow an attack upon his reputation to cloud his compassion. He would have been justified in punishing her, but he opted for comforting her instead. How kind of him!

He also didn't lash out at the religious leaders' prejudice. Since they caught this woman in the act, why didn't they drag along the man?

We have opportunities almost daily to react to situations judgmentally or mercifully. It was Jesus' kindness that profoundly affected the situation for the better. Kindness may seem small, but it is a major attribute of love.

Background Bulb:

When Joseph first heard of Mary's pregnancy, he debated what to do. The law called for stoning. (See Deuteronomy 22:20–21; Matthew 1:19.) However, Joseph decided to be kind to Mary and break their engagement secretly so she wouldn't be punished. He married her only after being convinced by an angel that Mary's baby was the Messiah.

Sprout and Scatter:

Think of someone who needs your kindness. He or she probably doesn't deserve your compassion. After all, we're not doing anything unusual when we're kind to those who are kind to us. Reach out to that person and see how your kindness affects the situation.

Think about it:

What types of situations challenge your urge to be kind?

_____

_____

_____

Now that you understand that being kind is a way of showing love, how can you say, "I love you," to someone today?

_____

_____

_____

Prayer Pot:

Dear God, forgive my lack of kindness toward . . .

_____

_____

_____

_____

_____

"No act of kindness, no matter how small, is ever wasted."
—Aesop in *The Lion and the Mouse*

Love Suppresses Envy

Today's Seed

> "Love . . . does not envy . . ."
>
> 1 Corinthians 13:4c

King Saul scratched his head and wondered if what he'd heard could be true. A shepherd boy volunteering to go head-to-head with Goliath, the Philistine champion who paralyzed his entire army with a taunt? What could this kid possibly accomplish that all Saul's mighty men couldn't—besides getting himself killed? *Oh well,* Saul thought, *if it gets this brash kid off my back, let him go.*

But then, could the unthinkable really be happening? This unknown shepherd boy, this little David, had actually killed the giant. *Unbelievable!* Saul thought. *Well, now my kingdom can get back to normal.*

Everything was cool until the victory parade. That's when Saul noticed what the women were singing: "Saul has slain his thousands, and David his tens of thousands" (1 Samuel 18:7). This nondescript shepherd boy was getting more press than the king. Saul turned green. He became preoccupied, intent on murder, stopped obeying God, and lost his kingdom. His envy brought about his ruin.

Dig Deeper:

The Greek word for "envy" means "to have warmth of feeling for or against; an earnest desire to have." Our English word denotes a negative meaning: spite or seeking to degrade another person.

Envy is ugly. The very reason Saul should have loved David was the reason he envied him. Envy finds reasons to be jealous where there should be love, respect, and honor. Envy cannot eliminate the good, so it covers it with nasty accusations, much like moss slowly covers a damp tree trunk. Maybe that's why jealousy is called the green-eyed monster.

Jealousy turns our focus inward to our own shortcomings and blinds us to the needs and emotions of the people around us. Release envy so you can see through eyes of love and celebrate, rather than covet, the talents of others.

Weed and Water:

The next time you feel that twinge of annoyance at someone else's success, or that desire to put someone in her place, recognize it as envy rearing its ugly head. Remind yourself that envy leads to ruin, and love does not envy. It does not seek to degrade another person. Replace that pang of envy with a prayer of thankfulness for that person.

Sprout and Scatter:

Next time you need to act as referee between two "warring" parties, whether children or adults, consider what role envy might play in the dispute. Pray for the two sides. Find something about which to compliment both parties or thank them. Encourage both sides to do the same. Perhaps the dispute will resolve itself.

Think about it:

What makes you react with envy?

_____

_____

_____

_____

List some ways you can counter personal jealousy with
positive responses.

_____

_____

_____

Prayer Pot:

Dear God, forgive my envy of . . .

_____

_____

_____

_____

_____

_____

"A heart at peace gives life to the body,
but envy rots the bones."
—Proverbs 14:30

Love Is Not Proud

Today's Seed

"Love . . . is not proud."

1 Corinthians 13:4d

Lucifer was one of God's brightest angels. He was extremely beautiful and was probably one of the highest-ranking angels in heaven. But he lost it all. How?

Pride. Conceit. Disdain for others, especially God. Lucifer's position gave him power. He thought his close association with God meant that he was better than the other angels. He thought he could take his throne and place it over God's. He thought his talents would turn heads. He figured he deserved just as much as God deserved.

He thought wrong.

Pride causes us to think and act as if we are better than others. Pride makes us focus on ourselves, ignoring God's role in our lives. Pride demands that others submit to us and our wishes, disregarding God's will. Pride is mutiny against God. This is not—drum roll, please—love. Satan (Lucifer's new name after God kicked him out of heaven) and one-third of the angels of heaven who followed him, miscalculated just how destructive pride

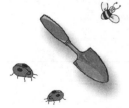

Dig Deeper:
The word "pride" carries with it the idea of inflation. When we are proud, we swell up with thoughts of our own greatness.

could be. Looking only at himself caused Satan to overlook the full power of God, and that led to his fall and destruction.

We may be talented, witty, educated, and well connected, but each of those characteristics is a blessing from God. When we're proud, we overlook the fact that God's love is responsible for every breath we take and every good thing in our lives. (See James 1:7.) When we take credit for our own talents and successes, we set ourselves up as gods. Our destruction will follow.

Background Bulb:

Genesis begins with the account of God creating the world. Satan appears in the third chapter. Satan's pride had brought about his fall from heaven some time prior (see Isaiah 14:12–15; Ezekiel 28:11–19), and now he was exercising his hatred for God by trying to get people to sin. Satan was temporarily successful until God sent Jesus to die, forgiving sin and providing a way for mankind to be rescued from its mutiny.

Weed and Water:

A reasonable amount of self-respect is healthy. There's a delicate balance, though, between a healthy self-image and conceit. We are usually blind to personal arrogance because we believe our own lies about ourselves. Isn't it interesting how skillful we are at identifying pride in others? Fall on your knees today and ask God to show you where you are proud. Consider asking a good friend to let you know if your view of yourself is unbalanced.

Think about it:

List three things pride makes us think or do.

_____

_____

_____

In what areas are you proud?

_____

_____

_____

_____

_____

Prayer Pot:

Lord, show me my pride and weed it out of . . .

_____

_____

_____

_____

_____

"A man's [or woman's] pride brings him low, but a man of lowly spirit gains honor."
—Proverbs 29:23

Love in Friendship

Today's Seed

> "A friend loves at all times, and a brother is born for adversity."
>
> Proverbs 17:17

Most of us have numerous acquaintances. We know the people with whom we work, our second cousins and great-aunts, people in our church, neighbors, our kids' playmates, and the clerks at the bank, post office, grocery store, and other places of business we frequent.

On the contrary few of us have numerous friends. Of all the people you know, who could you call at 3 A.M. when you're wringing your hands over a problem? Friendship is a bond of affection and trust accompanied with companionship and intimacy. Acquaintances are a dime a dozen, but true friends are priceless.

The Bible tells about the friendship of David and Jonathan. Jonathan loved David as himself (1 Samuel 18:1) and he showed his feelings in his words and actions.

When King Saul, Jonathan's father, was determined to hunt down and kill David, Jonathan helped David escape. Their friendship was bound by a covenant of love that was stronger than

Dig Deeper:
A friend and a brother are equals in today's seed because they are both faithful in times of trouble.

blood ties. David and Jonathan also encouraged each other to seek God and to live righteously. Although he knew David would be king in his place, Jonathan was willing to serve David (1 Samuel 23:17). Jonathan even risked his own life to protect David just as Christ laid his life on the line for us. This is the ultimate demonstration of love in friendship.

Friends are there for you in good and bad times. They keep you accountable. They want what's best for you. A true friend is love in action.

Weed and Water:

Would someone feel comfortable calling you for help at 3 A.M.? Are you dependable and honest? Can you keep a confidence? Are you genuinely happy when good things happen to your friends? Do you think or speak critically of others, or are you an encourager? Pray to God for the love and faithfulness to be a friend who can be trusted through adversity.

Sprout and Scatter:

Some friendships are meant for a specific season of life. Sometimes friendships pass away when the season is over, leaving only memories. Other times relationships might fade when our lives get busy and we neglect our friends. This week plan some time to spend with your best friend. Contact three friends you have neglected and invite them for tea or coffee. Have fun together remembering old times.

Think about it:

How was Jonathan a good friend to David?

_____

_____

Define a good friend.

_____

_____

How do you match up to that description?

_____

_____

Prayer Pot:

Lord, thank you for friends. Help me be a good friend by . . .

_____

_____

_____

_____

_____

_____

Make new friends, but keep the old,
One is silver and the other gold.

Love through Service

Today's Seed

"For Christ's love compels us, because we are convinced that one died for all, and therefore all died. And he died for all, that those who live should no longer live for themselves but for him who died for them and was raised again."

2 Corinthians 5:14–15

We have probably all seen a play, movie, or television show in which one person saves another person's life. Humorous productions often make use of this situation. The laughs start to roll when the character who has been saved tries to pay back the rescuer.

We see the grateful recipient going out of his way to serve, assist, and cajole the rescuer, often stumbling into more predicaments and occasionally needing to be rescued again. This gives the poor rescuer more work to do, and it gives the person being rescued more reason to repay the rescuer.

As we stumble through life, we are much like the bumbling actor in need of rescue from certain harm. We make mistakes. We pray. God comes through with mercy. We neglect to do what we

Dig Deeper:

The word "compel" comes from a Greek word *sunecho*, meaning "to arrest." The New Testament does not use this word to imply forced compliance, but the compulsion within our hearts to respond to God's love.

should and get ourselves into another mess. We pray. God comes through with forgiveness. Christ reaches out to us again and again with his never-ending forgiveness and love. His untiring willingness to come to our aid produces in us the desire to repay him through service of our hearts, minds, and bodies.

Today's seed emphasizes what our response to such a gift should be—to thank him and willingly give ourselves to our Savior. Even a lifetime of service could never repay what Christ has done for us by dying in our place. But he doesn't hold this over us in a threatening way. Instead, he draws us to himself through his love.

Background Bulb:

Today's seed talks about Jesus dying for all people. In the sacrificial system of the Old Testament, the blood of bulls and goats only temporarily covered the sins of the people. Jesus was the final sacrificial lamb. His death served as a permanent sacrifice for our sins and freed us from everlasting separation from the Father God.

Weed and Water:

Think about where you might be or what you might be doing without God in your life. Now think about what it cost God (the life of his Son) to bring you to himself. We should follow Christ's perfect example as we serve the Lord and serve others. Are you joyously repaying your debt of love with your service?

Think about it:

Name three things God's love has done for you.

- _____
- _____
- _____

What do you do in response to God's love?

_____
_____
_____
_____
_____

Prayer Pot:

Lord, help me show how much I love you by . . .

_____
_____
_____
_____
_____
_____

"Therefore, I urge you, brothers, in view of God's mercy, to offer your bodies as living sacrifices, holy and pleasing to God—this is your spiritual act of worship."   —Romans 12:1

Fear, Be Gone

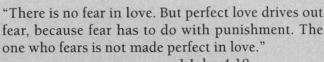

"There is no fear in love. But perfect love drives out fear, because fear has to do with punishment. The one who fears is not made perfect in love."

1 John 4:18

The number one thing people fear is speaking in front of an audience. Fear of death is rated number two. You may be able to avoid public speaking, but unfortunately the current death rate is 100 percent. None of us will escape it. Even Jesus didn't escape death.

Christians, however, have a surefire guarantee that snatches the fear out of the concept of death. The love of God allowed death to grip Jesus so it couldn't permanently grip us. God's perfect act of love took away the threat of eternal suffering and replaced it with the joyous hope of eternal life.

We may have to pass through death physically, but we will live again. And we don't have to fear meeting God on the other side of this life because he won't judge us by our sins. Jesus' death took care of that debt. Since God's love enables us to face death and beyond, we can face other things we fear and overcome them, too.

Are you single and afraid of living the rest of your life alone?

Dig Deeper:

The fear mentioned here does not mean awe or reverence for God. Reverence will increase as our love for God grows.

God's love casts out this fear because he has promised never to leave or forsake you. Are you afraid of financial struggles? God's love combats this too because he has promised to supply all your needs.

God's perfect love casts out all our fears as we learn to trust him. Christian speakers will even tell you that his love has cast out their fear of public speaking. If God is calling you up to the lectern, you can go without fear.

Weed and Water:

Take an inventory of your fears. In column one, list each of them. In column two, write down the likelihood and probable timetable for that fear to be realized. In column three, record the worst-case scenario if that fear materialized. In column four, write down what God's Word says about the alleviation of that fear. Now let the love of God drive out the fears expressed in column one.

Sprout and Scatter:

Even as you are assured of God's forgiving love, reassure the people close to you that they need not fear losing your love. Talk calmly with your children before and after meting out their discipline or punishment. Speak kindly to your spouse, coworkers, friends, or neighbors after a disagreement. Your loving response can strengthen the relationship, or perhaps catch the eye of someone who doesn't know Christ. That person might ask the reason for your love, giving you a chance to share about Christ's sacrifice that took your fear away.

Think about it:

What are you afraid of?

_____

_____

How has fear paralyzed you?

_____

_____

What foolish action have you taken as a result of fear?

_____

_____

_____

Prayer Pot:

Lord, help me to relax in your love when I am fearful of . . .

_____

_____

_____

_____

_____

_____

"Nothing is so much to be feared as fear."
—Henry David Thoreau

Joy Takes Action

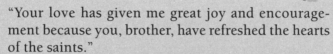

*Today's
Seed*

> "Your love has given me great joy and encourage-
> ment because you, brother, have refreshed the hearts
> of the saints."
>
> Philemon 1:7

True joy expresses itself in action. Joy is not simply a feeling of tranquility or a warm, fuzzy sensation. Joy is active and moving. Joy expresses itself in small gestures like writing a note of encouragement or smiling at a stranger, and in bigger acts of service and self-sacrifice like caring for an aging parent.

Joy finds fun and fulfillment in every simple task. Joy helps a new neighbor move in. Joy makes cookies for someone for no special reason. Joy picks up the telephone and calls a lonely person. Joy sings while vacuuming. Joy notices the beautiful floral patterns on dirty dishes. Joy volunteers for cleanup duty. And joy spills over into the lives of others.

From the context of Paul's letter to Philemon, where we find today's seed, we see that Philemon actively helped the members of the church that met in his home. His energy and actions were a blessing to all including Paul, who was encouraged to see this

Dig Deeper:
The Greek word *anapano* is translated "refreshed." It has also been translated "rest." When we help others, our actions give them an opportunity for rejuvenation.

brother help others so diligently. But Paul appealed to Philemon to do one more thing: welcome his former slave Onesimus back home with love and friendship. Onesimus had run away. Philemon could have had Onesimus arrested or executed. Instead, Paul asked Philemon to treat Onesimus as a brother. Encouragement and support are actions of joy, but the most joyous action of all is forgiveness and reconciliation.

Weed and Water:

Busyness alone does not bring joy. The source of joy lies in the motivation and focus behind our endeavors. Only activities that lead us to caring for others will generate joy. We will never find joy or contentment in selfish acts—only dissatisfaction and boredom. The surest path to joy is to lose ourselves in a cause greater than ourselves. As you move through this week, ask yourself a question: why are you doing what you are doing? If you don't like your answer, pray for a change of heart and move forward in joy.

Sprout and Scatter:

The reports of Philemon's joyous actions gave Paul great joy. When we let our joy show by taking action, we not only help the people we minister to but also the spectators who observe us. With this double blessing of joy, we should wake every day asking ourselves: "What can I do today to bring joy into someone's life?"

Think about it:

What is your attitude when you do good deeds?

_____

_____

_____

_____

_____

Name three ways you can bring joy to someone.

_____

_____

_____

Prayer Pot:

Lord, fill me with joyous intentions to . . .

_____

_____

_____

_____

_____

The roots of joy grow deepest in the soil of service.

Joy in Witnessing

Today's
Seed

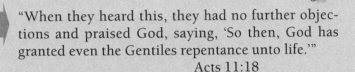

"When they heard this, they had no further objections and praised God, saying, 'So then, God has granted even the Gentiles repentance unto life.'"
Acts 11:18

If you have ever been part of helping a friend discover Jesus, then you understand what caused the disciples to praise God in today's seed. When they heard the news that Gentiles had been saved, the disciples and Jewish Christians were overjoyed.

Perhaps there is no greater joy than seeing a friend open his or her heart to Jesus in faith. Suddenly emptiness is filled and desperation disappears as a person turns toward the light of God. Sometimes you can actually see the change in a person's face. Smiles and twinkling eyes replace worry lines. People who are generally quiet suddenly have something to say.

When Jesus enters a life, all wrong behaviors are not instantly erased. Long-lasting change will take time, regardless of the person's desire to honor the Lord. Spiritual maturity develops from spending time alone with God, studying his Word, and exercising self-discipline. But in spite of the often difficult process of altering

Dig Deeper:
Doxazo is the Greek word translated "praised" in today's seed. It means to render esteem or give honor. Give all the glory to God when you see a soul enter Jesus' family.

behaviors, new believers have a special zest and enthusiasm for spiritual things. Their joy is contagious.

The disciples experienced great joy when they saw the Gentiles find salvation because they knew the peace and joy that they themselves had found. To see a friend come to know Christ reminds us of the freedom we have in our own salvation. We understand that the new life in Christ is not only a happier existence on earth but also a future life in heaven with the Lord.

Background Bulb:

The Jews were astonished to learn that the gospel message was for Gentiles, too. In traditional Jewish thought, Gentiles were subhuman. God surely could not love them. When the apostles learned that salvation was for Gentiles, they could have reacted with disgust or anger. Instead, they reacted joyfully. Later, some Jewish Christians tried to force the Gentiles into following Jewish traditions like circumcision and dietary rules. In the beginning, though, the leaders of Christianity, especially the apostles, praised and worshiped God for the salvation of the Gentiles.

Sprout and Scatter:

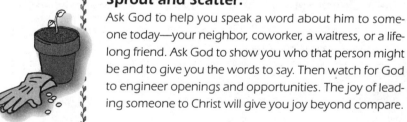

Ask God to help you speak a word about him to someone today—your neighbor, coworker, a waitress, or a lifelong friend. Ask God to show you who that person might be and to give you the words to say. Then watch for God to engineer openings and opportunities. The joy of leading someone to Christ will give you joy beyond compare.

Think about it:

Describe how you feel when you tell others about Christ.

_____

_____

_____

_____

Who might God be asking you to witness to?

_____

_____

_____

Prayer Pot:

Lord, lead me to the person that needs you and help me to . . .

_____

_____

_____

_____

_____

_____

"Those who bring sunshine into the lives of others cannot keep it from themselves."
—James Barrie

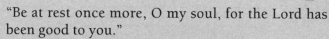

Joy Found in Resting

Today's Seed

"Be at rest once more, O my soul, for the Lord has been good to you."

Psalm 116:7

On Sunday in Europe, almost all the shops are closed. Couples and families walk slowly down the streets peering into shop windows. They read books in the park and play quiet games together. In Israel families spend *Shabbat*, the Sabbath, talking to friends and family. They eat a late, leisurely breakfast that was prepared the day before.

Contrasted to the hustle and bustle of weekends in the United States, the slow pace overseas is astonishing. We spend our days off running errands. We even turn our playtime into work—lugging laptops along on vacation, or passing up an evening of solitude to meet with a personal trainer. We have forgotten the value of rest.

How can Christians rest in the middle of a restless lifestyle? According to today's seed, we must simply make the decision to withdraw and recuperate. That's what Jesus did. Crowds followed Jesus everywhere. Multitudes gathered around him begging for

Dig Deeper:

The word "rest" comes from the Hebrew word *menuwchah*. It means a place of quiet. Rest in the mercy and power of God.

miracles. The pressure was constant, so he recommended rest to his disciples. "Then, because so many people were coming and going that they did not even have a chance to eat, he said to them, 'Come with me by yourselves to a quiet place and get some rest'" (Mark 6:31).

We can choose to relax because the God who made and controls everything knows we need periodic rest and quietness. He wants us to slow down and take a breather. He not only cares about us, but also loves to bless us with good things. Now that's something you can climb into your recliner to contemplate!

Weed and Water:

Let's face it. We all have a million things to do. In all the busyness, we often forget to focus on or even spend time with God. Make time today to rest and listen. Take a walk alone. Find a place to hide out where you can read your Bible and pray for a few minutes. Relax and do what the psalmist did—remind yourself that God has been good.

Sprout and Scatter:

Do you know a child who is constantly pursuing endless activities and projects? As you discover the joy of rest, share your discovery with the children in your life. Take them on leisurely walks. Read a book or listen to a tape together. Look at pictures and talk. Your conscious effort to slow the pace of life could change the future, one child at a time.

Think about it:

What activities or projects are keeping you from rest?

_____

_____

What do you need to do to commit to a regular time
for relaxation and rest?

_____

_____

What do you think are the benefits of rest?

_____

_____

Prayer Pot:

Lord, remind me to rest today when I . . .

_____

_____

_____

_____

_____

_____

"There is no joy in the soul that has
forgotten what God prizes."
—Oswald Chambers

Joy in Times of Trouble

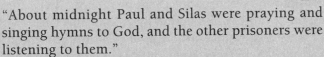

Today's Seed

> "About midnight Paul and Silas were praying and singing hymns to God, and the other prisoners were listening to them."
>
> Acts 16:25

While Paul and Silas were on their missionary trip, they encountered a slave girl who was plagued by evil spirits. They freed the girl from the spirits, and in doing so got in big trouble with her owners. The spirits had enabled the girl to predict the future, and she had been profitable to her owners. However, without the spirits she was an ordinary girl with no moneymaking tricks. Her furious owners filed charges and dragged Paul and Silas to jail.

How would you react if you were falsely accused and jailed? Would you fuss and fume? Would you doubt God and wonder if he had forgotten you?

Even though Paul and Silas were beaten, harassed, and jailed, they did not shake their fists at the authorities or at God. Instead, they let joy shine through their trouble. They praised God in prayer and song despite their chains.

Joy in times of trouble is only possible when we focus on God

Dig Deeper:

"Singing hymns" comes from the Greek word *humneo*, which means "to celebrate." Paul and Silas were not pretending or putting on a show. They were truly cheerful.

rather than trials. Think about it—Paul and Silas were praying and singing! Their actions seem unbelievable in light of their physical situation. We visualize them in a damp, dirty dungeon with their wrists and ankles bound by chains. But Paul and Silas focused on their spiritual situation. They thought about how Christ had freed them from the chains of sin and lifted their souls out of the filth to be washed white as snow. Even in physical chains, they knew they were free men. With that thought foremost in your mind, wouldn't you sing along?

Background Bulb:

Today's seed tells us the other prisoners in the jail that night listened. Paul and Silas impacted the prisoners so much that when an earthquake released their chains later that night, no one ran away. They wanted to stay close to the joy of Paul and Silas.

Weed and Water:

In John 16:20b, Jesus says, "Your grief will turn to joy." To illustrate, Jesus tells of a mother in labor. During labor she focuses on the end result—her baby—and that makes her pain worthwhile. By focusing on our end result—eternal fellowship with Jesus—we can endure the pain of this world with joy. Lay your troubles at Jesus' feet. He'll put joy into your arms.

Think about it:

What difficulties do you face today?

_____

_____

What do you do when you face troubles?

_____

_____

How can your grief be turned into joy?

_____

_____

_____

Prayer Pot:
Lord, give me a prayer and a song today when I face . . .

_____

_____

_____

_____

_____

_____

The truly happy person is the one who can enjoy the scenery on a detour.

Weeping Turned to Joy

*Today's
Seed*

"He who goes out weeping, carrying seed to sow, will return with songs of joy, carrying sheaves with him."
Psalm 126:6

Today's Bible seed draws a sharp contrast between weeping and joy. Weeping is a product of sorrow and despair. We shed tears of pain of the death of a loved one, a broken relationship, or even a lost opportunity. Sometimes we are overwhelmed by the magnitude of our trouble. We don't understand what God is doing or why he allows us to suffer so severely.

But the psalmist says he who goes out weeping will return with songs of joy. What makes the difference in the person? What changes his weeping into joy? The difference is that the weeping person went out with "seed to sow."

A seed represents a new beginning and a new life. Botanists tell us that when a seed is dropped into the earth, it dies. However, from the germ within the seedpod, a new life begins. The old seed disappears and the new life works its way up through the soil toward the light.

When we suffer pain and trauma, the best way to overcome grief is to sow a seed in another person. The act of dying to ourselves

Dig Deeper:

The Hebrew word translated "joy" is *rinnah*. It not only means happiness and gladness but also to shout about the joy. When our weeping turns to joy, we want the world to know.

breaks the hard shell of human self-centeredness. It hurts, but when we care more for others than for ourselves, weeping becomes joy. And God will bless our actions, multiplying our joy in the lives of others so that our planting results in sheaves of thanksgiving and happiness.

Weed and Water:

Strange as it may seem, weeping can be an expression of joy—just ask any mother at her daughter's wedding. When your heart is so touched by the magnitude of the moment, you may shout in celebration or you may flow with tears. Either way is a valid expression of joy. The next time you find yourself weeping with sadness, look at that moment as a chance to sow a seed. In the midst of your pain, take action to reach out in kindness to another, and see how God blesses your efforts.

Sprout and Scatter:

Sowing seeds of joy into another person requires us to be aware of what is happening in that person's life. When someone is having difficulties, we can help by being a good listener. We can remind them of the power and faithfulness of God. And when their sorrow turns to victory we can join them and shout for joy, sing songs of celebration, and cry tears of joy.

Think about it:

When has God turned your sorrow into joy?

_____

_____

_____

_____

Name three people that you can reach out to with seeds of joy.

_____

_____

_____

Prayer Pot:

Lord, help me shout for joy today when . . .

_____

_____

_____

_____

_____

Joy is in the heart, not the circumstances.

Joy Unites

Today's Seed

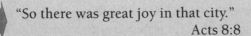

> "So there was great joy in that city."
>   Acts 8:8

The local TV station broadcast the good news that a kidnapped nine-year-old girl had been found alive. All of the family and neighbors gathered to celebrate. The many volunteers who had searched for days came back to headquarters one more time to share the excitement.

They had a reason for joy. The child, who had been lost and feared dead, was alive! A police officer found her locked in a hotel room fifty miles away. For five days, search and rescue professionals had combed the area with little hope. No doubt each person thought about the awful dangers the child might face. They imagined that the missing child was their own son or daughter, and fear for her safety was felt by everyone in the area. But when the girl was found alive and unharmed, joy united the city.

In today's seed when Philip went to a city in Samaria and told the people about Christ, they believed. Many paralytics and cripples were healed. The good news of physical and spiritual healing

Dig Deeper:

The word "joy" in today's seed is from the Greek word *chara*, which means calm delight. Learning the good news of Jesus Christ brings deep inner joy.

united the whole city. No doubt the townspeople recounted tales of their lifelong fears and remembered how dark the future had seemed. Before meeting Philip they felt hopeless. But his message about Jesus Christ introduced new, refreshing hope unto the people's lives, and they delighted in their new freedom and joy. They were unified in celebration.

Background Bulb:

The gospel spread from its beginnings in Jerusalem outward into Samaria and beyond. Prior to Philip's visit to Samaria, the Jewish Christians in Jerusalem had experienced trouble. Stephen, one of their leaders, had been brutally killed by the local authorities. Other leaders had been imprisoned. The rest of the Christians had run for their lives. They fled to cities outside Jerusalem. As they ran, they told everyone they met about Jesus and his great love. They experienced joy despite their former persecution and current displacement.

Sprout and Scatter:

The disciples' persecution caused them to travel to many parts of the world, and as a result, the gospel was brought to you and me. When we face troubles and experience Christ's help in dealing with them, do we tell everyone we meet about Jesus and his great love for us and for them? Joy is a uniting force, because with joy comes hope, and everyone is hungry for hope. Share about God's work in your life. This is the key to bringing joy and unity to our city.

Think about it:

What can I do to bring joy to my friends and neighbors?

_____
_____
_____

How would my city be different if it were united in joy about Christ?

_____
_____
_____
_____

Prayer Pot:

Lord, show me how I can bring joy to my city today by . . .

_____
_____
_____
_____
_____
_____

Joy is like potato salad—when shared with others it's a picnic.

Joy in the Bible

Today's Seed

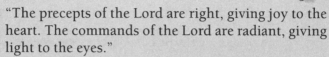

> "The precepts of the Lord are right, giving joy to the heart. The commands of the Lord are radiant, giving light to the eyes."
>
> Psalm 19:8

A story in the Old Testament Book of Nehemiah helps us understand today's Bible seed. The Israelites assembled in the town square. Ezra, the scribe, brought out a scroll containing the treasured law of Moses. He stood on a high wooden platform where everyone could see and hear him. As he began to read, the people all stood up, lifted their hands, and responded, "Amen, Amen."

The law of Moses is the first five books of the Bible. The reading probably took several hours. Though they must have been tired, the people responded with great joy.

What is it about the Bible that makes our hearts glad and our steps lively? According to today's seed it is because the Word of God is right.

Righteousness and justice are referred to as a plumb line (Isaiah 28:17). When you hang wallpaper and your walls are not perfectly straight, you must drop a plumb line—a chalky, weighted

Dig Deeper:

The term "giving light" in today's seed is from the Hebrew word *owr*, which means luminous as when the sun first comes up. Hearing God's Word is invigorating like the break of day.

string that hangs straight and provides you with a point of reference. Without it, you will have a crooked wrinkled mess on your wall.

The Bible is like that plumb line. Through it, we have access to God's instructions—straight and true. When the whole world seems topsy-turvy, we have the accurate Word of God to lead us. When we want to know what is right or wrong, the Bible gives us the answer. God's plumb line brings us great joy because with it we can recognize the value or danger of new trends, ideas, or sinful excesses.

Weed and Water:

How can we become more interested in and in love with the Bible? Jeremiah said, "When your words came, I ate them" (Jeremiah 15:16). To Jeremiah, knowing God's Word was as important as eating. He had experienced the joy of obedience. We can do the same. Immerse yourself in Scripture each day. Get an easy-to-read translation that will bring the words alive on the page. Discover as Jeremiah did, that "they [the words] were my joy and my heart's delight."

Sprout and Scatter:

Do you know someone who doesn't have a Bible? You could change his or her life by giving them one. Pick a good, readable translation. Mark the Roman road to salvation (Romans 3:23; 5:8; 6:23; 5:1; 10:9–10; and 10:13) with a highlighter. Write the person a note asking them to read the Book of John and then call you to discuss it. This simple act could change their life for eternity and bring great joy into their world.

Think about it:

What right thing have you learned from the Bible that brought you joy?

_____

_____

_____

What do you think are the benefits of reading the Bible for longer than five minutes at a time?

_____

_____

_____

Prayer Pot:

Lord, help me carve out time today to read your Word by . . .

_____

_____

_____

_____

_____

_____

True joy can be sought, thought, or caught, but never bought.

Parental Joy

Today's Seed

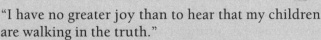

> "I have no greater joy than to hear that my children are walking in the truth."
>
> 3 John 1:4

Ah! The birth of a baby. Mother and Father have planned for that fabulous moment when the birthing room is suddenly filled with the exclamations: "It's a boy!" or "It's a girl!" Such joy is hard to duplicate!

After birth comes the parenting. Just to hear a child say a first word or understand a new concept is such fun. To see a child's successes on the athletic field or in the classroom makes a parent's heart swell. It's great to watch your child follow Christ—from the first step of salvation to his continuing growth in Christian character.

But no joy is greater than to hear someone else tell you that your child has demonstrated Christlike character at a time when you were not present. Then you know that your child has made the Lord's principles his or her own.

John wrote today's seed in his third letter and addressed it to a man named Gaius. Gaius was John's friend and apparently had

Dig Deeper:

Though translated "walk," the Greek word *peripatoeo* also means to live as a companion. Walking in truth means living side by side with Christ.

been kind and loving toward others as well as to John. When John heard a good report about Gaius from others, John was overjoyed. John uses the words "my children" often in his letters because he took a personal interest in younger believers. He loved to encourage his spiritual children, and they made him feel like a proud parent.

Weed and Water:

Your children will become more Christlike if they see that you are like Christ. People evaluate Christianity and Christ by what they see in us. We need to ask ourselves some serious questions: *Will my children and my coworkers want to be Christians because they see so much love and joy in me? Will my children know to take their doubts and worries to Christ because that is what I've done? Will others trust Christ in times of difficulty because they have watched me do that?*

Sprout and Scatter:

To experience the joy of watching your children grow spiritually, guide them early in life by exposing them to the Bible and to Christian friends and activities.

If you don't have children, you can still experience parental joy by getting involved in a mentoring relationship. "Adopt" the children of a single parent. Be a Big Sister. Volunteer to listen to a child read at a local school. Offer to baby-sit in your church nursery one or more Sundays a month.

Think about it:

How and when do you talk to your child about Jesus Christ?

_____

_____

Name four things about yourself that would make someone else want to be a Christian.

🐞 _____

🐞 _____

🐞 _____

🐞 _____

Prayer Pot:
Lord, may my children walk in the truth by . . .

_____

_____

_____

_____

_____

Instead of making choices for your children, teach them how to make choices for themselves.

Surprised by God

Today's Seed

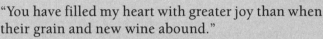

"You have filled my heart with greater joy than when their grain and new wine abound."

Psalm 4:7

Dream Vacations. We all love to plan and organize a holiday—a few days away from stress and difficulties.

But Americans tend to take vacations that are more stressful than relaxing. We drive too far, try to see too many attractions, snap too many Kodak moments, and spend more money than we intended.

When we arrive back home, we are more haggard than when we left. Unfortunately, we discover that the planning and anticipation brings us more joy than the actual trip.

David, the writer of today's seed, reminds us that although work—in his case harvesting grain and making wine—brings satisfaction and vacations bring respite, it is God who brings joy. God-given joy is deeper and lasts longer than good times in the past or dream vacations.

We don't have to travel to exotic islands or ski extreme slopes to gain a new frame of mind or new energy. God is always with us to refresh, revitalize, and reenergize us.

Dig Deeper:

The psalmist used the Hebrew word *sameach* for "joy." It could also be translated "glee"—like the glee of a child who has been surprised. Open your eyes with delight at the things of God.

All we have to do is open our eyes to the unexpected delights around us. A sunrise of pinks and purples. A bush blooming with colorful flowers. A baby's laugh. A telephone call from an old friend. A kind word from a coworker. With God ordinary days are days of joy. Surprising, isn't it?

Background Bulb:

The teachings of Jesus are surprising when compared to common wisdom. Jesus said that the last shall be first—we rush to the front of the line. Jesus taught that to gain your life you must lose it—protecting our turf is our number one goal. Jesus said you must give away your wealth to be rich—we hoard our resources. Jesus knew the way to joy and taught surprising principles to show us the way.

Weed and Water:

If you haven't felt surprised by God lately, examine your schedule and your attitude. Are you too busy? Have you allowed negative thoughts, complaints, and pessimism to overshadow your sense of fascination and delight? Resolve now to do away with cynicism and embrace wonder. Think of a person or situation that has caused negative emotions in your life lately. Ask yourself, *how is God blessing me through this?* Ask God to open your eyes to his surprises.

Think about it:

What did you do on your most memorable vacation?
Name a recent surprise from God.

_____
_____
_____

What teaching of Jesus surprises you?

_____
_____
_____
_____

Prayer Pot:

Father, forgive me for failing to see your miracles. Help me to
open my eyes to . . .

_____
_____
_____
_____
_____

Joy is found in living each day as if it
is the first day of your honeymoon or
the last day of your vacation.

Joyful Worship

Today's Seed

> "Speak to one another with psalms, hymns and spiritual songs. Sing and make music in your heart to the Lord."
>
> Ephesians 5:19

Have you ever been in the mountains on a clear winter day? As far as you can see, snow-covered peaks climb high toward the sky. Evergreens dusted with powdery snow point upward. The magnificence of that outdoor cathedral overwhelms you and you want to break into song, "How Great Thou Art!" or "What a Mighty God!"

Worship is recognizing and magnifying God. It is our response to his greatness and his character. When he displays himself in nature, we worship his power and goodness. When he speaks through his Word, we worship the depth of his wisdom. When he moves in our lives, we worship the intensity of his kindness. Worship can be quiet or loud. It can be private or public. But there is no true worship without joy.

Joy is often expressed in music and dance. Miriam sang and danced with joy as the Israelites started toward the Promised

Dig Deeper:

Psallo is the Greek word translated "make music" in today's seed. It means to applaud with music. Our God is so awesome, we should clap.

Land. David wrote and sang psalms of joy and thanksgiving. He danced before the Lord when the ark of the covenant was brought back to its rightful place. Mary sang when the angel announced the coming of Jesus. The early Christians sang as they met together. In heaven we will sing a new song (Revelation 5:8–9).

We may not all be skilled at dancing or musically gifted. We may not even be able to walk or carry a tune, but God doesn't care if we sound or look good. He just loves the sight and sound of a joyful Christian praising and worshiping him.

Weed and Water:

Worship is a reflection of our attitude about God. If you are not joyful about worshiping, you may need an attitude-and-gratitude check. Do you love and honor him? Is he the one you turn to for help or comfort? Do you recognize that all things—the fun and the difficult—come from him? The joy of worship is only possible when our hearts are focused on God. Ask him to give you a spirit of joyful worship.

Sprout and Scatter:

You can influence others to worship joyfully. Don't be bound by rules or traditions. Point out the gorgeous sunrise to your husband or carpool group. Show your children the pretty butterfly on a wildflower. Praise God with your voice. Sing aloud. Clap your hands. Open your heart to the joy of spontaneous worship. Your joy will help others realize what an awesome God we serve.

Think about it:

What is your favorite hymn or praise chorus? Why?

_____

_____

When have you sung it privately in celebration of our mighty God?

_____

_____

How can you make your worship of God more joyful?

_____

_____

Prayer Pot:

Father, I worship and adore you. Give me a song today when . . .

_____

_____

_____

_____

_____

_____

She who forgets the language of worship can never be on speaking terms with joy.

Real Beauty Starts with Peace

Today's Seed

"Instead, it [your beauty] should be that of your inner self, the unfading beauty of a gentle and quiet spirit, which is of great worth in God's sight."

1 Peter 3:4

Have you noticed the beautiful young women in TV programs and ads? The multimillion-dollar entertainment industry equates youth with beauty. The cosmetic industry attempts to provide us with all the creams and cover-ups necessary to keep us looking young—and therefore more beautiful according to pop culture.

God's beauty measurement has nothing to do with appearance. When God measures, he puts the tape around the heart, not the face or hips. And he doesn't count birthdays. He looks into our hearts. If he sees a gentle and quiet woman, he admires the real beauty found deep in the soul, not on the surface of the skin.

What is a gentle and quiet spirit? It is a woman with a deep, abiding sense of security who knows the Father of the universe loves her. It is a woman who is inwardly calm because she knows God is in control. From that knowledge come peaceful actions. The gentle, quiet woman is a woman of peace. She chooses not to

Dig Deeper:

The Greek word for "unfading" is *aphthartos,* which means it will not decay or deteriorate. The peace of God is a beauty secret that lasts a lifetime!

be irritated by others because God is in control, and she chooses not to provoke others because she is secure. Her choices in turn nurture peace in the lives of those around her. Such a woman is truly beautiful.

We may never be on TV or be asked to endorse a product, but if we have peace because of our trust in God, we are beautiful women.

Background Bulb:

Today's seed is part of a larger message from Peter that begins, "Wives, in the same way be submissive to your husbands . . ." (1 Peter 3:1–6). The media scoffs at the idea of a wife being submissive. The cynics are correct when they say that wives have strength and rights. We do have the power to be demanding and we can usually get our way. But when we choose to submit to our husbands, we relinquish our power, choosing instead to develop the beautiful trait of peace.

Sprout and Scatter:

One of the best ways to tell others about Christ is to let them see how he affects our lives. Display peace in your day-to-day routines as well as in trying circumstances. When a careless driver cuts you off, resist the temptation to express anger. When you receive bad news, give the situation to God rather than surrendering to anxiety. A peaceful response stands out like a beacon of light in a chaotic world.

Think about it:

Describe a time when God changed your distress to peace.

_____

_____

_____

How can you become a more peaceful person?

_____

_____

_____

_____

Prayer Pot:

Lord, when I am annoyed today, please remind me that . . .

_____

_____

_____

_____

_____

_____

A peaceful woman is a rare and beautiful treasure.

The Peace of Letting God

Today's Seed

> "But as for me, I watch in hope for the Lord, I wait for God my Savior; my God will hear me."
>
> Micah 7:7

Sometimes it's hard to ask for help. Often our pride tells us we can do it better on our own. Sometimes we worry about being a nuisance by requesting aid. Perhaps we figure our burdens are ours to bear—if we ask someone to lighten the load, he or she will either do so grudgingly or flat out refuse, leaving us just as burdened as before, and humiliated to boot.

Depending on God is different than depending on people. We shouldn't hesitate to ask him for help. We can expect to be supported, defended, and rescued by him. All we have to do is let God take our burdens from us.

The phrase "I will watch in hope for the Lord" suggests that Micah, the writer of today's seed, has peace to wait because he trusts the Lord. Truly "letting God" means recognizing that there is no one else, even ourselves, in control.

How can we gain this kind of peace? The first step is trusting God, as Micah did. Our Lord is all-powerful and all-knowing—

Dig Deeper:

When the prophet said that God would "hear" him, he used the Hebrew word *shama,* meaning that God listens and is interested. When you pray to the God of the universe, he pays attention.

who better to trust? The next step is waiting. Let him do what he is going to do when he is ready to do it. Waiting isn't easy, but it is necessary. The last step is expecting God's best. Remember that his best may not be what we wish for, but his best is always what we need.

Background Bulb:

Before Micah wrote the words of today's seed, he wrote about the situation around him. He was greatly distressed because of the wickedness of the people. The leaders of Israel were corrupt and the children were rebellious. He couldn't trust any person because no one lived with honor or integrity, so he turned to God. He found peace in trusting God and letting him do his will, even if it meant correction and punishment for the people of Micah's time.

Weed and Water:

Micah cried out, "What misery is mine!" (Micah 7:1). Then his cry changed to a voice of hope and rejoicing: "You do not stay angry forever but delight to show mercy" (Micah 7:18b). His tone changed from despair to joy and peace because he recognized God's control. He let go and placed himself and his future with the Lord, whom he could trust above anyone else.

Think about it:

Name one thing that you never let anyone help you with.

_____

_____

How can you turn it over to God?

_____

_____

How can you become more dependent on God?

_____

_____

Prayer Pot:

Lord, I will let you do your work in my life today, especially when . . .

_____

_____

_____

_____

_____

Let go and watch in hope as God orchestrates all.

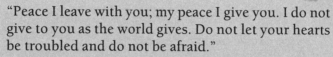

His Peace

Today's Seed

"Peace I leave with you; my peace I give you. I do not give to you as the world gives. Do not let your hearts be troubled and do not be afraid."

John 14:27

"Good morning." "Have a nice day!" "How are you?"

These popular phrases get tossed about in crowds, at checkout counters, and in elevators. We say the words as polite, emotionless chitchat and expect no response. What a surprise it would be if someone actually answered with a list of their problems and ailments!

In Jesus' day the common greeting was *Shalom* or "peace." Technically, it meant, "May you prosper in body and soul and enjoy earthly and heavenly good." Like our common greetings, shalom was an empty wish. Before Jesus went back to heaven, he promised to leave his followers with real peace, not mere formality or flattering words.

All of us start life in disharmony with God. Our natural condition of rebellion toward God causes turmoil within and wreaks

Dig Deeper:

The English word "give" is translated from the Greek word *didomi*. One of the definitions of this word is to furnish necessary things. Jesus knew that his peace would be necessary for our survival.

havoc without. Jesus could promise peace because "he himself is our peace" (Ephesians 2:14). Without Christ, true peace doesn't exist. Trying to find peace apart from Christ is like trying to breathe on Mars—the required elements just aren't there.

When we become Christ's followers, the wreckage of sin is repaired by inner peace—Jesus' peace. Calm and composure replace anxiety and ruin. Troubles and difficulties don't disappear, but we can deal with them because we have his peace.

Jesus' legacy included tranquility and happiness for the mind and soul. What a great way to part company!

Background Bulb:

Jesus is the author, prince, promoter, and keeper of our peace. When he was born, the angels sang, "Peace on earth." On the Sea of Galilee, he calmed the storm with his voice, saying, "Peace be still." On the cross, Jesus purchased our peace with his blood. He owns peace and has the power to give it. Just as he freely promised peace to his disciples, he offers his peace to us each day.

Sprout and Scatter:

Jesus gave us the ability to tell others about our peace with God. Set a goal to give up elevator talk and start giving out real blessings. When your friends are distressed, speak softly with words of encouragement. When you see a child crying, kneel down to his eye level and offer a hug. Visit a lonely elderly person. Bring him or her some fruit and talk about Jesus. Stay awhile, and leave in peace.

Think about it:

What is keeping you from the peace of Jesus?

_____

_____

_____

_____

_____

List some words of peace that you can begin to use in your daily conversation.

_____

_____

Prayer Pot

Lord, I ask you for your peace when . . .

_____

_____

_____

_____

_____

Where the Spirit of the Lord is, there is peace.

Peace for Jerusalem

Today's Seed

> "As he approached Jerusalem and saw the city, he wept over it and said, 'If you, even you, had only known on this day what would bring you peace—but now it is hidden from your eyes.'"
>
> Luke 19:41–42

From the Mount of Olives you can see a panoramic view of the beautiful city of Jerusalem. To see the magnificent ancient structures is an emotional experience. As Christ approached the city, he began to weep. He knew about the cross and the pain he would soon bear, but he didn't cry for himself. He cried because he could see that the city's future was bleak for many years to come.

There would be conflicts, wars, and finally destruction in A.D. 70. Jesus knew that over the centuries the Romans, Greeks, Turks, Muslims, Crusaders, and others would tramp through the streets. Today, the city is divided into sections for various groups. The tension is thick. There is no peace.

Jesus wept because the city would reject salvation and the opportunity for spiritual peace. The Jews wanted a king who would bring political peace. They were blind to the peace that Jesus offered—

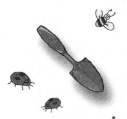

Dig Deeper:

The word "known" is translated from the Greek word, *egnoos*. It means to perceive or understand. We must open our eyes wide so that we are aware of his peace.

peace with God. Jesus wept because they didn't understand that peace was standing before them on the mountain.

The consequences of rejecting Christ are huge. He offers eternal life. If we miss him, we miss heaven. But he also offers peace while we live on earth. Our daily schedules, activities, responsibilities, and even our pleasures can hide him from our eyes and cause us to miss the peace he offers.

Background Bulb:

For centuries, God warned and pleaded with Israel to obey him. David repeated God's message in his songs: "If Israel would follow my ways, how quickly would I subdue their enemies and turn my hand against their foes!" (Psalm 81:13). Isaiah warned, "If only you had paid attention to my commands, your peace would have been like a river" (Isaiah 48:18). God did not hide peace from Israel. Their stubborn hearts blinded them to what was before their eyes.

Sprout and Scatter:

According to Bible prophecy, Jerusalem will not find total peace until Jesus returns. Until then, we can pray for the missionaries and Messianic congregations who are proclaiming the message of Jesus the Messiah. Though the city itself may not have peace, individuals can find peace in their hearts through the message taught by these groups.

Think about it:

What news articles have you read lately about the unrest in Jerusalem?

_____

_____

_____

How can you open your mind and heart to see God's peace?

_____

_____

_____

Prayer Pot:

Father, forgive my blindness. Open my eyes to . . .

_____

_____

_____

_____

_____

_____

"Pray for the peace of Jerusalem."
—Psalm 122:6

Contented Peace

Today's Seed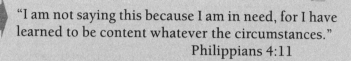

"I am not saying this because I am in need, for I have learned to be content whatever the circumstances."

Philippians 4:11

A magazine advertisement describes luxurious living: "All that is required is to be surrounded by dramatic furnishings assembled with regard to color, texture, and composition. This will create harmony and perfect balance."

No one would dispute how nice it is to be surrounded by beautiful furniture and accessories, but despite what this magazine ad promises, these things are not the key to peace and contentment.

Paul learned to be at peace no matter what the circumstances. We tend to think that Paul meant we have to live in poverty. But Paul makes it clear that he also means finding contentment in abundance too. "I know what it is to be in need, and I know what it is to have plenty. I have learned the secret of being content in any and every situation, whether well fed or hungry, whether living in plenty or in want. I can do everything through him who gives me strength" (Philippians 4:12–13).

Dig Deeper:

Paul's word "content" is translated from the Greek word *autarkes*. This is the only place in the New Testament where this word is used. It means independent of circumstances.

It didn't matter to Paul whether dinner was a feast or bread and water; he could be at peace. It won't matter if priceless antiques or early marriage hand-me-downs surround us, we can live luxuriously in God's peace. Only God can give the strength to continue without physical means. And only God can keep the greedy human heart from wanting more in times of plenty.

Peace is not enduring life with teeth clenched and jaws set. Peace is allowing God to give and withhold as he sees fit and to be at peace with his decisions.

Background Bulb:

Paul learned to be content. His formal education was grand by the standards of the day. He had studied under the great Jewish scholar Gamaliel. This tutor gave Paul all the skills and knowledge he needed to be successful. But contentment and peace had to be learned through experience. Every time God provided for Paul's needs, Paul gained peace. When God blessed Paul in ministry, it added peace. Learning at the feet of experience is an education indeed.

Sprout and Scatter:

You can show others how to have peace and contentment. Develop an attitude of satisfaction by enjoying life regardless of your number of possessions. Be content with what you have. Don't buy compulsively. When others see that you are satisfied, they will wonder why. Then you'll have the opportunity to explain how God can give them peace, too.

Think about it:

How far along are you in learning contentment?

_____

_____

_____

What can you do to help someone else find peace?

_____

_____

_____

_____

Prayer Pot:

Lord, forgive my dissatisfaction and give me peace and contentment today when . . .

_____

_____

_____

_____

_____

A contented peaceful mind is a continual feast.

Peaceful Heart

Today's Seed

> "A heart at peace gives life to the body, but envy rots the bones."
>
> Proverbs 14:30

From conditions as common as angina to obscure cardiac problems, heart disease is the number one killer of women. Surprisingly, women are more vulnerable to heart disease than men. In fact, each year 50,000 more women die from heart disease than men. Most women don't recognize the warning signs until they are in jeopardy. A healthy heart is vital to healthy living. Our physical heart pumps life-giving blood throughout the body. When a patient has a blockage, the doctors rush in to open clogged arteries.

The Bible speaks of our heart not as the physical organ in our chests, but as the spiritual control center of our lives. Our hearts think, feel, and decide. For a healthy heart, we need peace to flow into every part of our being.

Today's seed contrasts envy with peace. Funny how our peace is wrapped up in our desires, isn't it? If our desires are out of control

Dig Deeper:
The word "peace" translated from the Hebrew word *marpe* literally means "heart of health." If a heart is diseased, life cannot be rich, full, or long. A healthy heart, free from envy, is peaceful.

and we want what others have, we can't be at peace. We might pick another word to contrast with peace—chaos, busyness, or lack of money—but God chose the word envy because he knows that our peace is greatly affected by our attitude toward others who have been successful.

Envy is a cancer that eats away at the peace in our hearts. A healthy heart generates peace. Peace is found when we are pleased that God has blessed someone else with no thought of what he has or hasn't done for us.

Background Bulb:

Before Christ became our personal Savior, we had no chance for a peaceful heart. Sin, guilt, and selfishness controlled our actions and feelings. When we met Christ, he came to dwell in our hearts through faith (Ephesians 3:17). He also "put his Spirit in our hearts as a deposit" (2 Corinthians 1:22). With Christ residing in us and the Holy Spirit guarding the door, peace reigns in our hearts.

Weed and Water:

Good and bad all start in the heart. Fear, love, courage, anger, joy, sorrow, and hatred are born there. Our spiritual consciences thrive or fail in the atmosphere of our hearts. Our prayers should be to let only good generate there. "Do not be anxious about anything, but in everything, by prayer and petition, with thanksgiving, present your requests to God. And the peace of God, which transcends all understanding, will guard your hearts and your minds in Christ Jesus" (Philippians 4:5–7).

Think about it:

What emotions or desires keep you from peace?

_____

_____

_____

_____

What triggers envy to form in your heart?

_____

_____

_____

_____

Prayer Pot:

Lord, clean out the debris of my heart. Bring peace in . . .

_____

_____

_____

_____

_____

_____

"Let the peace of Christ rule in your hearts."
—Colossians 3:15

Peacemakers

Today's Seed

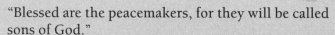

"Blessed are the peacemakers, for they will be called sons of God."

Matthew 5:9

Terrorists devise dastardly plots to kill thousands. Newspapers are filled with talk of war. Differing ethnic and religious groups clash violently. Sometimes a world leader or statesman travels halfway around the world to help two bickering groups avert war. The statesman may work nonstop for days in an effort to broker peace. If he is successful he is hailed as a hero—a peacemaker.

When Jesus used the word "peacemakers" he wasn't talking about truce-makers who negotiate for warring parties to lay down their guns, nor did he mean the absence of war. He was referring to peacemakers who bring the peace of God—the only true peace—to the world.

Peacemakers are at peace with God because of his forgiveness of their sins. Because of God's mercy toward them, they forgive and overlook offenses of others, and thus promote peace among human relationships. Peacemakers also bring God's peace to those around them by spreading the gospel.

Dig Deeper:

According to the *International Standard Bible Encyclopedia,* the Greek word translated "peacemakers" would be more descriptive if it were translated "peaceworkers." We are blessed when we become entrepreneurs of peace.

When we are saved, we become God's children, and children inherit traits from their parents. Jesus promised that peacemakers would be called the sons of God. As God's children, we are to take on his peaceful nature and show others how to cooperate instead of fight. The family resemblance shows; our actions mark us as children of God.

God's peace is greater than any treaty professional negotiators could sign. God's peace is so great it's beyond understanding. Yet it is profoundly simple. If world leaders offered the peace of God, there would be peace indeed.

Background Bulb:

The common practice among the Pharisees of Jesus' day was to show your righteousness by how you dressed and what rules you followed. But Jesus was more concerned with inner devotion to God than external appearances. A true peacemaker examines motives and intent, not superficial actions.

Sprout and Scatter:

We may not be summoned to a faraway country to negotiate world peace, but God calls us to become diplomats in our families, neighborhoods, and churches. We can promote peace by using the peacemaking techniques of Jesus. He was merciful, gracious, and long-suffering. When we forgive, old family disputes are settled. When we are helpful, neighborhood quarrels are resolved. When we refuse to grumble, church disputes disappear and unity is restored. Use your inner peace, influence, and wisdom to end wars and introduce reconciliation.

Think about it:

Describe a "warring" situation in your church, neighborhood, or family.

_____

_____

_____

How can you promote peace in that situation?

_____

_____

_____

_____

Prayer Pot:

Lord, show me where I can be a peacemaker today by . . .

_____

_____

_____

_____

_____

_____

Peace may cost as much as war but it is a better buy.

Sleep in Peace

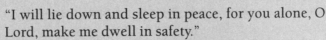

Today's Seed

"I will lie down and sleep in peace, for you alone, O Lord, make me dwell in safety."

Psalm 4:8

One third of all adult Americans—about 50 million people—complain about their sleep. Some are insomniacs who cannot sleep longer than a few minutes at a time. Others sleep long hours and find it difficult to become alert and functional. Still others suffer from sleep apnea in which they sporadically fail to breathe while sleeping and jolt awake, gasping for breath.

Recent scientific research is beginning to provide answers for sleep problems that stem from medical ailments, but scientists agree that stress, worry, and anxiety often trigger insomnia and other sleep disorders.

Trying to fall asleep can be a nightmare when your body is at rest but your mind is wide awake. The house may be calm and quiet, but your thoughts race through the darkness: *How will I pay the bills? What if the baby gets sick? Is my teenager safe? How will I deal with the illness of my parent? Why does my marriage seem dull and lifeless? Did I do the right thing?"*

Dig Deeper:

The word "sleep" is translated from the Hebrew word *yashen*. It means to grow old. What an amazing thought! We can relax in God's safety for as long as we live.

Today's seed assures us that because God is responsible for our safety, we can sleep in peace. He protects and defends us against all enemies—those that threaten physical harm as well as nagging worries that rob us of rest. No disturbance is too big for him to handle. We are not alone, and we do not need to worry. We can rest peacefully with our Lord in control.

Background Bulb:

David was forced to hide from King Saul in the mountains of Engedi, a rugged and treacherous terrain. As Saul's army hunted for him, David and his men needed to be alert, yet they needed sleep. How could they rest when an army was trying to kill them? David's solution was to ask for God's protection and peace. "Answer me when I call to you, O my righteous God. Give me relief from my distress; be merciful to me and hear my prayer" (Psalm 4:1).

Weed and Water:

If you have trouble sleeping, don't keep trying. Stop staring at the clock and get up. Fix yourself some warm milk, and jot down all the things that are running through your head. Pray and give those things to God. When you go back to bed, try praying or reciting Scripture until you fall asleep. How sweet is our sleep when all our difficulties are in God's hands.

Think about it:

List some peaceful things you can do to relax before you go to bed tonight.

_____

_____

_____

What fears do you need to relinquish to God so that you can sleep in peace?

_____

_____

_____

Prayer Pot:

Father, remind me of your peace and help me to sleep when . . .

_____

_____

_____

_____

_____

_____

"When you go to bed at night, rest in peace because God is still awake."
—Victor Hugo

Forgiveness Brings Peace

Today's Seed

> "If it is possible, as far as it depends on you, live at peace with everyone."
>
> Romans 12:18

When a pond sits with no outlet and no fresh water flowing in, it gets stagnant. Anger is like stagnant water—murky, dark, and smelly. Anger sits on our heart, festering and polluting until it destroys our peace and takes us prisoner.

Sometimes we try to hide our angry feelings in something that sounds more spiritual—righteous indignation. Secretly we believe that the person we can't forgive should pay for what he did. The fellow who left his wife and children should be miserable with his new young family. The girlfriend who blabbed our deepest secrets should have her secrets aired in public too. The businessman who ripped us off should fail. The church member who promised to help but never showed up doesn't deserve our help now. We even get an odd satisfaction from seeing him or her suffer.

Anger and the desire for revenge take us captive, and no captive has true peace. True forgiveness is releasing the other person

Dig Deeper:

Two qualifiers in today's seed—"if it is possible" and "as far as it depends on you"—show that God understands that we will have conflict with others. We can't change people, we can only change our attitudes.

from punishment. We can experience the peace of forgiveness when we make a conscious effort to wish good things for the future of the person who hurt us. To wish that person happiness and success or to pray for God to bless his or her ministry is the essence of forgiveness.

The most amazing thing happens when we forgive. Suddenly, *we* are free! We are released from the bondage and captivity that pollutes our lives because of anger and resentment—free from the burden we carried around. In other words, we are at peace.

Background Bulb:

We don't deserve God's forgiveness. Each day our sins are many, yet he forgives us anyway. "His compassions never fail. They are new every morning . . ." (Lamentations 3:22–23). He has commanded us to offer his forgiveness to others. "Bear with each other and forgive whatever grievances you may have against one another. Forgive as the Lord forgave you" (Colossians 3:13).

Sprout and Scatter:

Misunderstandings, criticism, envy, and hurt feelings wreck our peace. But when we refuse to quarrel and learn to forgive others, we experience true peace. You can start by overlooking a person's fault's. If they are always late, don't stew and complain. Accept it, plan for it, and be at peace. With the help of the Holy Spirit, develop a forgiving heart.

Think about it:

What has someone done to you that you can't seem to forgive?

_____

_____

How can you change your attitude toward that person?

_____

_____

Write a one-sentence prayer asking God to bless that person.

_____

_____

Prayer Pot:

Lord, increase my peace by helping me forgive . . .

_____

_____

_____

_____

_____

Peace and forgiveness go together like a hand and a glove.

Practicing Patience

Today's Seed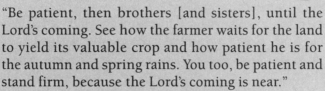

"Be patient, then brothers [and sisters], until the Lord's coming. See how the farmer waits for the land to yield its valuable crop and how patient he is for the autumn and spring rains. You too, be patient and stand firm, because the Lord's coming is near."

James 5:7–8

Have you ever wondered how a farmer remains patient when his whole livelihood is tied up in seed, soil, fertilizer, and rain? Nothing can be done to hurry the harvest. Once the seed is planted, nature takes over. All the farmer can do is watch and wait.

Today's seed exhorts us twice to develop patience. As the farmer anticipates that first ear of corn, he keeps busy with other chores even though his mind is focused on the fruits of his labor. He's patient, yet diligent, trusting that sufficient sunshine and rain will cause the crops to thrive.

His life, like ours, is based on faith. Since we cannot predict the future, we must trust God with the tiny seeds we have planted. Have you shared the gospel message with a neighbor? Rejoice!

Dig Deeper:

Huetos is the Greek word meaning "to rain." Water sustains all life: animal, vegetable, human, and even spiritual life. We are blessed by the refreshing rains of God's spirit.

That's one seed. Have you prayed with a friend whose husband needs healing? That's another seed. This may not seem like much today but when you consider the total number of seeds you sow in a lifetime, you can say, "Wow!"

Do you have loved ones for whom you are praying? If so, don't lose hope. God's Holy Spirit is the fertilizer that works in all of us. Sometimes we may not see results as soon as we'd like. Remember that you were once a tiny seed nurtured by a fellow gardener. Now you've grown into a healthy plant that will bear much fruit because of the water and fertilizer you received.

Weed and Water:

Patience is not easy to come by, is it? It's probably one of the most common struggles we face. The good news is that patience is an attainable character trait. When you face a situation that leaves you feeling impatient, pray for a way to keep your cool. The Holy Spirit will enable you to remain calm even when you want to take charge or bulldoze your way through.

Sprout and Scatter:

Planting spiritual seeds every day is not as difficult as it seems. When God provides you with an opportunity to speak, he will also give you the right words. Don't worry if you are not able to explain the whole plan of salvation. Just speak as much as the listener is willing to hear. Ask God to nurture the seed.

Think about it:

How can you yield those situations that require patience to God's control?

_____

_____

_____

Name three people that would benefit from your planting and watering spiritual seeds in their lives.

🐞 _____

🐞 _____

🐞 _____

Prayer Pot:

Father, let me be an example of patience as I . . .

_____

_____

_____

_____

_____

_____

"Knowing trees, I understand the meaning of patience. Knowing grass, I can appreciate persistence."
—Hal Borland

Patient Clothing

Today's Seed

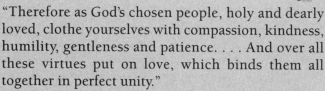

"Therefore as God's chosen people, holy and dearly loved, clothe yourselves with compassion, kindness, humility, gentleness and patience. . . . And over all these virtues put on love, which binds them all together in perfect unity."

Colossians 3:12, 14

If you've ever wondered who coined the phrase "patience is a virtue," you'll be pleased to know this little catchphrase has its root in the Bible.

If you're like most of us, you cringe every time you hear these words. Life would be much easier, we think, if we could pick and choose our virtues. Compassion is great, we say, because I love to prepare meals for shut-ins, but patience is too much to ask because that person makes me crazy.

Take heart. The Holy Spirit is at work in us to give us more patience. As we shouldn't bypass certain passages of Scripture, neither should we pick and choose which virtues to exhibit. This is why Paul, the author of today's seed, reminds us that love goes

Dig Deeper:
"Virtues" are not old-fashioned terms from the Victorian age; they are necessary for modern life. Virtues are noble and worthy thoughts, feelings, and actions. Other specific virtues include modesty, purity, and integrity.

over all these virtues and holds them together. Love is the final piece of "clothing" that completes our spiritual outfit.

Webster's Dictionary defines a virtue as a "particular moral excellence." All of the attributes in today's seed are necessary for the believer's new life in Christ. Living without patience is like forgetting to wear socks on a freezing cold day. We will be unprepared for the elements, particularly when a snowstorm hits. And if we're predisposed to fits of anger, the snowstorms will hit quite often.

Make it your priority to dress appropriately.

Weed and Water:

The wardrobe of the old sinful man has been destroyed. For example, if you had a temper before you became a Christian, visualize that habit as a piece of clothing that was burned. You now have a new wardrobe at your disposal. Each day this week as you dress, choose one piece of outer clothing and name it "patience." Picture yourself receiving this clothing from Christ and practice living up to its name.

Sprout & Scatter:

In Colossians 3:12, Paul wrote, "Bear with each other and forgive whatever grievances you may have against one another." He understood that forgiveness is a huge part of patience. Bearing with others, overlooking grievances, and forgiving like Christ forgave us will do much to make our world a calmer place. Forgiveness begets patience. And when we are patient with others, they become more patient with us.

Think about it:

If you could choose, which virtue(s) would you avoid?

_____

_____

How have your thoughts on patience been challenged?

_____

_____

_____

How will you put Paul's list of virtues into action?

_____

_____

Prayer Pot:

Dear Lord, forgive me for not wearing . . .

_____

_____

_____

_____

_____

Patience—don't leave home without it.

Patiently Soaring!

Today's Seed

"He gives strength to the weary and increases the power of the weak. Even youths grow tired and weary and young men stumble and fall; but those whose hope is in the Lord will renew their strength. They will soar on wings like eagles; they will run and not grow weary, they will walk and not be faint."

Isaiah 40:29–31

Eagles soar higher than most other birds. To do so they rely on thermals, which are rising currents of warm air and updrafts. Soaring is accomplished with very little wing flapping. Eagles conserve their energy and wait for the currents to do the work for them.

Unlike eagles, humans are notorious for flapping their "wings" in bustling activity. We don't like to wait. We prefer to forge our own paths through life's obstacles. Consequently, we get burned out.

Fatigue is a fact of physical life. Ministry or family crises can leave us drained. Our wings become heavy and flying is difficult. Should we just conjure up the strength to go on? No. The believer

Dig Deeper:

The phrase "shall renew" in verse 31 suggests an exchange of strength. We exchange our weakness for God's strength.

need not trust in his or her own sufficiency. God says, "I will renew the strength of those who hope in me."

When we are at the end of our strength, the secret to more power is in turning to the Lord and waiting. Hope means we expectantly believe God will do what he says. Like eagles, we need to wait patiently until God sends a fresh wind to move us in the direction he wants us to go. He has power that is never exhausted. We may faint and grow weary, but he upholds the whole creation. Relying on his wind, the believer soars upward toward God.

Background Bulb:

Isaiah 39 speaks of the capture and slavery that Israel would soon face in Babylon. During their captivity the Israelites imagined that God was too tired to help them, or he had forgotten about them. Chapter 40, from which today's seed is taken, tells of the hope and comfort God would bring to his people as they journeyed back to Jerusalem to repopulate their land. God wasn't expecting the people to have superhuman strength; he was expecting them to turn to him for renewal.

Sprout and Scatter:

We've all seen godly saints succumb to burnout. These are the gals who organize the church bazaar year after year with nary a hand to help them. They flap and flap when no one else rises to the occasion. If you notice a Christian friend heading in this direction, offer to share the responsibility or encourage her to wait for God's power. Take notice of those who are weary, impatient, or facing burnout and pray for them.

Think about it:

List two things about God that give you hope.

_____

_____

When do you sense your spiritual strength weakening?

_____

_____

What will you do today to exchange weakness for strength?

_____

_____

Prayer Pot:

Lord, bless me with patience and a fresh wind for . . .

_____

_____

_____

_____

_____

_____

Stop flapping your wings and wait on God.

Patience in Affliction

Today's
Seed

"To keep me from becoming conceited because of these surpassingly great revelations, there was given me a thorn in my flesh, a messenger of Satan, to torment me. Three times I pleaded with the Lord to take it away from me."

2 Corinthians 12:7–8

Do you have a disability? Have you recently been diagnosed with a disease? Do you live with pain?

If so, you can identify with Paul. He was afflicted with a physical ailment he referred to as his "thorn in the flesh." Some sources believe Paul had leprosy or another debilitating disease, perhaps an eye ailment. Whatever Paul's thorn was caused him enough bodily pain and mental anguish that he pleaded with the Lord to remove it.

In his wisdom, God chose not to heal Paul. God left the ailment intact so that Paul's character would grow and develop through suffering. Paul was humble enough to admit that he would have been conceited if God had not given him this thorn. Paul recognized that good could result from his illness or disability. Later,

Dig Deeper:
The word "affliction" is translated several ways in the Bible: persecution, trouble, harassment. The Greek word translated "thorn" here is used only once in the New Testament, making it difficult to know Paul's exact problem.

in verse 10 he said, "I will boast about my weaknesses, so that Christ's power may rest on me. That is why, for Christ's sake, I delight in weaknesses, in insults, in hardships, in persecutions, in difficulties. For when I am weak, then I am strong."

Obviously, Paul wished for complete health and physical strength, but he didn't use his suffering as an excuse for not doing God's will. He was thankful that God could strengthen his character in times of suffering and he got on with the business of living.

Background bulb:

Paul's patience or endurance was tested from the day of his conversion. He was long-suffering in the face of his various afflictions and trials such as imprisonment, beatings, and persecution. The end result was a humble servant who placed his trust in the Lord Jehovah and was a great role model for future generations. Paul wanted nothing less than to be used by God, whatever the circumstances.

Weed & Water:

We are all faced with ailments—physical diseases, emotional heartaches, or spiritual disappointments. Regardless of our personal "thorn in the flesh," we can take comfort in knowing that our afflictions are temporary. Earth is not our final resting place—heaven is. When we get to heaven God will wipe away every tear from our eyes. By focusing on that hope we will be comforted.

Think about it:

Name two of your current afflictions.

_____

_____

How patient are you in these troubles?

_____

_____

What good could come from these afflictions?

_____

_____

_____

Prayer Pot:

Dear Lord, I confess my patience is tested when . . .

_____

_____

_____

_____

_____

God is with you in suffering.

Patience with Christians

Today's Seed

"Be completely humble and gentle; be patient, bearing with one another in love."

Ephesians 4:2

Your neighbor drives his car into your trash can again! Aagh! *One of these days,* you think, *I'm going to run over his trash can and see how he likes it!*

Our patience is tested on a daily basis. We're tempted to act on our feelings, but then we remind ourselves that we can't expect non-Christians to act Christlike, and we calm down.

But today's seed isn't talking about being patient with unbelievers. It emphasizes patience within the body of Christ, reminding us to be humble, gentle, and loving toward our brothers and sisters in Christ. Why?

Often we expect Christians to act better than non-Christians. Then we are shocked and angry when they disappoint us. We become impatient. We let down our guard and vent our frustration. Our families often bear the brunt of our impatience. We think, *It isn't easy to live with those I love.* But it also isn't easy for those we love to live with *us.*

God knows that his children will have conflicting opinions and

Dig Deeper:
The word "bear," as in "forbearing," means to endure, tolerate, and put up with our fellow believers.

differing personalities, but he doesn't let us off the hook. Think back to an instance when you were expected to bear with someone who grated on your last nerve. By the end of the day, you may not have liked that person or yourself. Most likely the feeling was mutual. That's why Paul emphasizes the importance of patience. No matter how much we all desire to glorify God, we will annoy each other at times. Patience allows us to bear with one another in love and work through our differences.

Background Bulb:

Christ set the standard of bearing with one another during his earthly ministry. Daily he listened to and put up with ordinary men and women who experienced doubt and weakness in their faith, needed repeated reminders about the simplest things, argued over who among them was the greatest, and jumped to the wrong conclusions. His response was never anger, but always patient forbearance.

Weed and Water:

Assume that you will "blow it" from time to time. When you do, apologize for your impatience. The disciples sat at the feet of the Messiah, but they messed up too. Christ will forgive you when you seek him. Ask the Holy Spirit to help you act with patience as a humble servant and not a hothead. Study the four Gospels to see how Jesus reacted when people got under his skin. Then try to follow his example.

Think about it:

Describe the last time you lost your patience.

_____

_____

_____

Who witnessed your impatience?

_____

_____

_____

What should you do about the situation—even if no one saw you?

_____

_____

_____

Prayer Pot:

Lord, forgive me for not living patiently with . . .

_____

_____

_____

_____

Those who live with us know if Christ is living in us.

God's Patience with His Children

> "Yet the Lord longs to be gracious to you; he rises to show you compassion. For the Lord is a God of justice. Blessed are all who wait for him!"
>
> Isaiah 30:18

A traffic jam. Cars and passengers sat bumper to bumper. In one car sat a mother and a child of about three strapped to a car seat. The child was crying at the top of his lungs. Tears poured down his face. A few books and a stuffed animal lay scattered about him. His mother stared straight ahead, seemingly unconcerned about the screaming thirty-five-pound monster in her backseat.

How like that young child we are when we want something from God that we can't or shouldn't have! We want to plow through life, yet sometimes God engineers events to place us in a spiritual or emotional traffic jam. While we sit there, God gives us many blessings. Yet we toss aside the "books and stuffed animals" and cry our little hearts out, demanding more. Nothing God does for us is satisfactory because we want that one thing we can't have.

The child in the car didn't understand about the traffic jam. His mother was doing all she could to help him. Eventually, they

Dig Deeper:

The Hebrew word *chakah* is defined as "wait for" or "longs for." God longs for us to calm down, so we can enjoy his blessings while we wait.

would arrive at their destination and he would climb out of his seat. While he cried, his mother waited patiently. We don't always understand God's actions. Although we cry pitifully, God waits patiently, knowing that he will bring us safely to our destination. He has much patience with his children.

Background Bulb:

Isaiah chapter 30 describes Israel's "temper tantrum" against God. The nation was in trouble, but instead of seeking help from God, they asked Egypt to help them do battle. Egypt's help was useless. The battle was a disaster. Yet God waited patiently while the people of Israel learned their lesson. Today's seed tells how God longed to comfort his children and give them blessings if they would trust in him.

Sprout and Scatter:

God is always ready to forgive our tantrums. Despite our childlike foolishness he is merciful and patient. We can use God's example and power to show similar patience to others. Obviously we'll never be perfect—but we can remember how patient God is with us and ask him to help us become more patient with others. Picture yourself or the person who is giving you problems as the child in the traffic jam. Ask yourself, "What would Jesus do?"

Think about it:

Describe a time when you behaved toward God like the child in the traffic jam.

_____

_____

_____

What did God do in response?

_____

_____

_____

_____

Prayer Pot:

Dear Lord, forgive my foolish demands. Teach me . . .

_____

_____

_____

_____

_____

_____

Pray for God's patience and watch for blessings!

End of God's Patience

Today's Seed

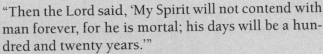

"Then the Lord said, 'My Spirit will not contend with man forever, for he is mortal; his days will be a hundred and twenty years.'"

Genesis 6:3

God's patience with unbelievers lasts only so long before he pronounces judgment on evil or wrongdoing. He does not become impatient as we do, but God is just and must judge evil because of his nature, not because he's had it with us.

Today's seed is God's spoken word to Noah. In Noah's day corrupt lifestyles were the norm. The people had lost all desire for a relationship with God and had forgotten his promises. Martin Luther and others teach that God gave these godless people 120 years to get their acts together. That was more than a man's life span. You'd think that would be more than enough time for them to return to the Lord.

While God waited, he gave the sinful people a visual warning. He told Noah and his sons to build a massive boat. While Noah sawed boards and hammered nails, he warned the people and urged them to seek God's salvation. But they laughed at Noah and

Dig Deeper:

The Hebrew words for "contend" and "judge" are almost identical in meaning. The word means to govern in all areas. God is in complete control.

his message. After 120 years had passed, God spoke again to Noah, saying, "I am going to put an end to all people, for the earth is filled with violence because of them." And God shut Noah and his family safely inside the ark.

When the rain started to fall, the people realized God was serious. But it was too late. They perished. God pronounced judgment because the people had turned their backs on him and wholeheartedly embraced a wicked lifestyle. His patience with sin has a limit. His justice was doled out in Noah's day and will be again at Christ's Second Coming.

Background Bulb:

Biblical names carry realistic meanings. Noah's name implies that he walked with God. In all the earth, only this man's family was spared from the floodwaters that destroyed all living things. Noah was not perfect or sinless, but he was righteous in his relationship with God. Because of his love for Noah, God spared Noah's family and enough animals to replenish the earth.

Sprout and Scatter:

When God judges humankind in the last days, the unsaved will perish. Unfortunately, just like in the days of Noah, the unsaved today do not believe God will judge them. They often react harshly toward God and *blame* him if we mention eternal judgment. That's when our patience has to kick in. We must forgive their anger and rejection, and continue to love them and pray for their salvation.

Think about it:

Why does God judge evil?

_____

_____

_____

_____

How is his punishment different from ours?

_____

_____

_____

_____

Prayer Pot:

Dear Lord, I trust your perfect justice, but I plead for your
patience toward . . .

_____

_____

_____

_____

Regard God's patience as salvation.
Without it we all would be lost.

Our Patience with God

Today's Seed

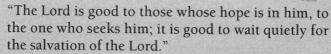

> "The Lord is good to those whose hope is in him, to the one who seeks him; it is good to wait quietly for the salvation of the Lord."
>
> Lamentations 3:25–26

Lines at the bank. Lines at the grocery store checkout counter. Lines at the restaurant. Lines at the theater box office. Some days it seems all we do is wait for other people to hurry it up. We want everything in life to move along according to our schedule, and when it doesn't we lose patience.

Unfortunately, our impatience with *life* carries over into our relationship with God. We pray for healing, financial blessing, the salvation of a loved one, or answers to life's tough questions.

At first we are patient and willing to wait on God's timing because we have read that his ways are higher than ours. We watch expectantly for the answers to our prayers to materialize. But as time passes, we grow impatient. We pray, "Lord, why are you taking so long to answer? Haven't I been faithful in asking your will for my life? Could you hurry it up (just a little), Lord?"

Dig Deeper:

The Hebrew translation for "wait quietly" is *duwman* and means dumb, or silent. This does not imply that God expects us to be unintelligent, but merely silent enough to hear his voice.

When an answer doesn't materialize immediately, we wonder if God hears and if he cares. We begin to doubt that God has our best interests at heart. Hope vanishes.

Instead of waiting quietly, we complain. Today's seed tells us that it is good to wait quietly, without ranting and raving. Quietness is not the enemy; it enables us to seek God and listen for his leading.

Weed and Water:

God is the Alpha and the Omega, the author of time. He acts on our behalf when the time is right; he is never late. God's timing will always be to our benefit, causing us to stretch and to bear spiritual fruit. Start writing down your prayer requests. Each week review the list and keep track of which prayers have been answered. Over time you will develop a deeper understanding of God's timing in your life.

Sprout and Scatter:

We can encourage those around us to wait on the Lord for answers to prayer, especially as we experience God's faithfulness in our own lives. Perhaps you were protected from a bad situation. Looking back, do you see how your character and closeness to God developed as you waited? Share those examples with others.

Think about it:

When you wait quietly, what *aren't* you doing?

_____

_____

_____

_____

Name two examples of how waiting turned into blessing for you.

🐞 _____

🐞 _____

Prayer Pot:

Lord, grant me the wisdom to understand your timing in . . .

_____

_____

_____

_____

_____

_____

_____

God's timing is perfect.

Consequences of Impatience

Today's Seed

> "Then Sarai said to Abram, 'You are responsible for the wrong I am suffering. I put my servant in your arms, and now that she knows she is pregnant, she despises me. May the Lord judge between you and me."
>
> Genesis 16:5

As women, wives, and mothers we are often tempted to help our husbands, children—and God—"get on with it" by running ahead of them and trying to make things happen.

Sarai (later named Sarah), Abram's wife, did just that while she waited for God to give her a child. God had promised that Abram's offspring would be as numerous as the stars. After waiting for the fulfillment of that promise while her biological clock ticked away, Sarai took matters into her own hands. She presented Abram with a substitute wife, one of her Egyptian slaves named Hagar. Abram slept with Hagar, who conceived and bore a son called Ishmael.

In giving Hagar to Abram, Sarai set into motion consequences that could never be retracted and created a source of strife that

Dig Deeper:
Sarai claimed her husband was responsible for her *chamac,* the Hebrew word meaning violence, cruelty, damage, or injustice. In addition to her sin of impatience, Sarai created strife in her marriage.

continues today. When she realized she was pregnant, Hagar despised Sarai. In response Sarai mistreated Hagar until the slave ran away into the desert. Sarai blamed the problem on Abraham—she was so creative! We would never have thought to do such a thing, right?

God took care of Hagar and Ishmael, yet he allowed Ishmael to become the father of the Arabs with whom Israel has conflicts even today. When Sarah finally gave birth to Isaac at the ripe old age of ninety, she must have looked back with sorrow on her lack of patience.

Weed and Water:

When we are impatient, God will forgive us. He forgave Sarai and later changed her name to Sarah, which signifies a lady or the princess of a multitude. He has the power to help us change. Stop to consider the consequences of the shortcut you are tempted to take by asking these questions: *Will it hurt me? Will it hurt anyone else? Will it hurt my relationship to God?*

Sprout and Scatter:

Children with Attention Deficit Disorder are taught to write down their "brilliant ideas," listing pros and cons before they act. Recovering alcoholics are told to call their support person when they are tempted to have a drink. Consider using the same strategies to conquer impatience. Asking someone in your family to hold you accountable may help that person learn to be more patient as well.

Think about it:

Name some consequences of Sarai's impatience.

_____

_____

_____

When are you impatient?

_____

_____

List some possible consequences of your impatience.

_____

_____

Prayer Pot:

Lord, forgive my impatience over . . .

_____

_____

_____

_____

_____

_____

Sometimes God allows us to take the long road home.

Patient Endurance

*Today's
Seed*

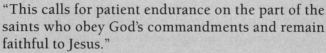

> "This calls for patient endurance on the part of the saints who obey God's commandments and remain faithful to Jesus."
>
> Revelation 14:12

"That's it! I'm not going back to school, Mom. It's too embarrassing!" Your twelve-year-old daughter stomps out of the room. Yesterday, her closest friends laughed when she announced her intent to join the morning Bible Club. Your daughter's humiliation is real. The Christian life is hard. At twelve, she is only beginning to learn what identifying with Christ means.

The longer we live the Christian life the more we ought to expect rejection from the world. Rejection hurts, and when it happens it calls for patient endurance. As we mature we learn that the ability to persevere does not come because we are smart or strong, but because of God's power working in us. From that experience we gain greater faith for the trials ahead. Our patience grows. Our hope lies secure in the knowledge that we will spend eternity with our Lord and Savior Jesus Christ. We have been promised the crown of life if we persevere (James 1:12).

Dig Deeper:

What we "endure" for Christ is temporary. One Greek translation for "endure" means to remain, to undergo, bear trials, or to persevere—to be patient in circumstances.

The secret to enduring persecution can best be summed up as trust and obedience. When the Lord returns we want to be found living for him. As we experience hardships for his name's sake we become like him in his suffering. Believers from every corner of the earth are being persecuted, and some will die for their faith. We are called to continue on until our trials cease or Christ returns.

Weed and Water:

Are you in the midst of persecution right now? Unsaved family members or coworkers may taunt you for your faith. The gospel is foolishness to those who don't believe. Pray that their understanding will be opened. Meanwhile, stand firm in your faith whether it is popular or safe to do so. Your eternal reward is on its way.

Sprout and Scatter:

As the last days approach, Christians are to bind together and encourage one another to live as Christ lived. We cannot allow ourselves to become lazy in our faith or our witness to the world. If you notice a brother or sister in Christ wavering, speak the truth in love to bring him to repentance. Don't be impatient—endure!

Think about it:

What makes living for Christ worth trials or persecution?

_____

_____

_____

Why must a believer patiently endure?

_____

_____

What will carry you through your trials?

_____

_____

Prayer Pot:

Lord, I cannot endure this life on my own. Help me . . .

_____

_____

_____

_____

_____

_____

"Life's trials will seem so small when we see Christ."
—Esther Kerr Rusthoi

The Art of Kindness

Today's Seed

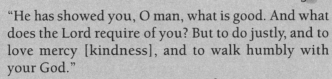

"He has showed you, O man, what is good. And what does the Lord require of you? But to do justly, and to love mercy [kindness], and to walk humbly with your God."

Micah 6:8

Has anyone ever warned you about something but you ignored the warning? Adults don't like to be told what to do even when the instructions given are for our own good.

The prophet Micah spoke truth to the people in Israel (the northern kingdom) and Judah (the southern kingdom.) He warned political figures and military leaders that judgment was coming. Even though their society appeared healthy, they were godless.

In Micah's day, kindness was a lost art. Wealthy oppressors stole land and homes by fraud. They dreamed such schemes while they slept. Israel and Judah's people worshiped idols even though they knew God was a jealous God. They treated each other and the Lord with contempt.

God delivered on Micah's warnings—partially at first, then completely about a century later when the Israelites were conquered and killed or taken into slavery by Babylon.

Dig Deeper:

"To love mercy" originates from the Hebrew word *checed* and carries the basic idea of freely and willingly showing kindness to others. God asks that we be his instruments of kindness in a fallen world.

Today's seed explains that God expects his people—leaders and average people alike—to be just, kind, and humble. A decay in our individual values saps our nation's strength and vitality. Our attitudes and actions toward others have a direct result on how outsiders view God. If we fail to show kindness to others, why should they listen to our words about Jesus' love and sacrifice? Judeo-Christian ethics no longer appeal to unbelievers when they see our hypocrisy firsthand. Micah's warning still applies.

Background Bulb:

The name "Micah" means "Who is like God?" The theme of the Book of Micah is godliness, and the message still has relevance today. God judged the Israelite nations in Micah's day, and he will judge all people finally and completely when Christ returns. As Christians we want to learn how to be like God by having a heart that responds to God and others in humility and kindness.

Sprout and Scatter:

The basis for our kindness is the mercy God has shown us. This is what we pass on to others. A good witness requires that we walk the talk and drop our holier-than-thou attitudes. Christ's mercy and forgiveness are all that separate us from the world. Only when we live according to God's Word will we have a godly influence in our homes, our society, and our world.

Think about it:

Name two sins in Israel and Judah's day.

_____

_____

What does God require of you according to today's seed?

_____

_____

In what ways are you failing to obey these warnings?

_____

_____

Prayer Pot:

Dear Lord, keep me close to you by . . .

_____

_____

_____

_____

_____

_____

Kindness should never be out of style.

Neighborly Kindness

Today's Seed "But a Samaritan, as he traveled, came where the man was; and when he saw him, he took pity on him. He went to him and bandaged his wounds, pouring on oil and wine. Then he put the man on his own donkey, took him to an inn and took care of him."

Luke 10:33–34

Your neighbor's husband lost his job six months ago and hasn't found another job. Their children's clothes are getting shabby and torn. Besides that, the children are always using your kid's toys and eating your food. It's easy to get annoyed. How should a Christian respond?

Jesus told a parable to show us how we are to treat everyone, even people we don't like. In the parable a Jewish man was robbed, beaten, and left for dead along a dangerous highway. A priest and a Levite both passed the bleeding man without stopping. Then a Samaritan man—an ethnic group hated by the Jews—stopped to help.

Both the priest and the Levite were unwilling to get involved because it would have cost them time, energy, personal safety,

Dig Deeper:

"Took pity" implies a deep feeling of sympathy that was far different from the other travelers. The Samaritan saw human worth in the hurt Jewish man.

money, and a change of attitude. Their attitude of avoidance was easier but not justified.

As believers we are to treat others with kindness like the good Samaritan. We are not to ignore needs or to look down our noses at those whose situations differ from our own. Kindness is behaving toward others the way God has treated us.

When God places a need before you in plain view, pray about whether he wants you to meet that need. If you feel the Holy Spirit leading you to act, give without expecting anything in return.

Weed and Water:

Scam artists take advantage of people's feelings of sympathy or kindness. They love to target older people who have money in the bank. If you receive phone calls or knocks on your door by strangers telling you they need money now, jot down their name and their organization's name, address, and phone number, and say you will contact them if you decide to help. Don't let them pressure you into acting immediately. Pray about their appeal over several days or weeks. Ask your family or friends to help you evaluate the request. Never give out your credit card or bank account number.

Sprout and Scatter:

We don't have to feel like being kind before we act with kindness. Feelings often follow action. Teach your children to be kind and to reach out to other children—even those who are difficult to like. Ask them if there is someone in their school class who needs kindness, someone who is different, ignored, made fun of, or a bully. Then brainstorm ways you and your children can show kindness to that child. Choose one act to try.

Think about it:

What did the Samaritan do to show kindness?

_____

_____

Why was the Samaritan able to demonstrate kindness?

_____

_____

What blessings might come from helping those in need?

_____

_____

Prayer Pot:

Lord, let me see the worth of others and . . .

_____

_____

_____

_____

_____

Kindness notices the beauty and worth of others.

Kindness ▪ 126

Hospitality

Today's Seed

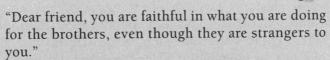

"Dear friend, you are faithful in what you are doing for the brothers, even though they are strangers to you."

3 John 1:5

In today's seed Gaius, a believer, is commended for his acts of hospitality toward the early church. He developed a reputation for being a gracious host to traveling teachers and missionaries.

Hospitality is just one form of kindness that we can show other believers, but it is a great service. As Christians we have a unique bond in Christ with all believers. If you have ever been alone in a foreign country or sitting shoulder to shoulder on a crowded subway you know the instantaneous bond that occurs when someone says to you, "Are you a believer?"

Use these God-given opportunities to be kind to fellow Christian strangers. Don't be afraid to invite new friends in Christ to your home or your neighborhood Bible study. Pay particular attention to visitors to your church; it's so easy to only talk with your circle of friends on Sunday morning. Reach out to newcomers and make them feel welcome.

Dig Deeper:

The word "hospitality" as used in Romans and Hebrews is *philoxenia*, meaning the "love of strangers." The word comes from the root *phileos*, which means a brotherly kind of love.

Show kindness to believers who are strangers by opening your home to traveling missionaries, church singers or drama teams, and exchange students. By volunteering to provide housing for such special guests, you will benefit from the gifts of these talented people. Call them in advance to inquire about their special needs. Offer to pray with them before their performance. A simple act of kindness often builds a spiritual bond that lasts a lifetime. Before you realize it, this stranger will be a friend.

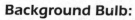

Background Bulb:

There were no Holiday Inns for traveling preachers or missionaries in the early church. Other believers housed Christians, often for weeks on end. Being hospitable involved sacrifice and inconvenience. Gaius, one of John's many children in Christ, is commended in today's seed for opening his home and heart.

Sprout and Scatter:

Be on the lookout for those who may be lonely, such as senior citizens, college students, or divorced parents within your church. Single parents are especially vulnerable—feeling like a third wheel at most church-sponsored events. Share a meal with a single-parent family. College and career singles love a home-cooked meal and may relish sharing the clatter and activity of a family with children. If you are hesitant, start small with an invitation for dessert.

Think about it:

Is it hard for you to reach out to strangers or new acquaintances? Why?

_____

_____

_____

How can you show kindness to strangers in a way that best uses your spiritual gifts?

_____

_____

_____

Prayer Pot:

Lord, let me hear the Holy Spirit when he gives me opportunities for . . .

_____

_____

_____

_____

_____

Kindness flows from love, which binds all virtues together.

Merciful Kindness

Today's Seed

> "I, even I, am he who blots out your transgressions, for my own sake, and remembers your sins no more."
> Isaiah 43:25

Kindness entails more than being nice to people we admire and respect. That's easy. Godly kindness involves mercy. Mercy means showing compassion, especially to someone who has offended us. It takes a conscious, deliberate act of our will. And that can be hard—even excruciatingly difficult.

Living for God is not just pretending to be kind or paying lip service to forgiveness of others. If we are to be holy as God is holy, then we must demonstrate the very character he breathed into us. We do this by going the extra mile to forgive when our feelings get hurt or when a friend we trusted with a confidence betrays us. There is no Scripture that excuses the Christian from forgiving as Christ forgave us.

Think of how many times a day God forgives. Psalm 103:10 says that God "does not treat us as our sins deserve or repay us according to our iniquities." We deserve punishment and anger for the ways we behave. We deserve to spend eternity in hell. Our

Dig Deeper:

The Hebrew word for "blot" is *machah*, which means to wipe off or remove. Picture someone wiping a bowl clean and turning it upside down so it can't be refilled. How precious is God's forgiveness of sins!

shortcomings and stubbornness must cause God great disappointment, but he reacts in love, even as he disciplines us. God has a perfect memory, yet he chooses to blot out or wipe clean our slate. He bestows forgiveness as an act of his kindness and mercy.

Background Bulb:

Jesus' life personified kindness and forgiveness. If any person ever had a justified reason not to forgive or not to be kind, Jesus did. When Jesus came to save mankind from their sins, he was mocked, beaten, spit upon, stripped, and nailed to a cross. What a grudge he could have held against humankind! Instead, as he breathed his last, he asked God to forgive his persecutors for their treatment of him. Jesus remained kind until the end.

Weed and Water:

God is pleased when we forgive and choose not to hold others' offenses against them. Next time that annoying person hurts you, mentally put the offense in a bowl. Take a paper towel or sponge and wipe the bowl clean. Then turn it upside down and place it where you can see it. When you are tempted to remember the offense, look at the upside-down bowl. You can't refill it! That issue is over.

Think about it:

Why is it difficult to forgive those who have sinned against us?

_____

_____

_____

How do you feel when you think of God's kindness toward you?

_____

_____

_____

Prayer Pot:

Lord, my struggle with forgiveness is never ending. Help me to be mercifully kind to . . .

_____

_____

_____

_____

_____

When you forgive, forget the sin forever.

Kindness Versus Selfishness

Today's Seed

"But mark this: There will be terrible times in the last days. People will be lovers of themselves, lovers of money, boastful, proud, abusive, disobedient to their parents, ungrateful, unholy, without love, unforgiving, slanderous, without self-control, brutal, not lovers of the good."

2 Timothy 3:1–3

One chocolate doughnut remains. Your out-of-town adult guests are busy packing. The children—all six of them—are playing upstairs. It's just you and the doughnut against the world. You win!

Just as you finish wiping the chocolate off your mouth, a guest appears in the kitchen and says, "I didn't have breakfast. Where's that doughnut? I'll just have that."

Oops!

We are all guilty of being selfish, putting our wants above others' wants, hoarding our money or possessions, or bragging about our latest raise or our kids' accomplishments. If selfishness is defined as acting according to one's own interests and needs with-

Dig Deeper:

"Lovers of themselves" is the Greek word *philautos,* which does not mean one who simply loves herself, but one who loves herself *too much*—to the point of being conceited and selfish. It means one who desires things to be easy and pleasant for herself.

out regard for the needs of others, then kindness is treating others the way we would like to be treated. (See Luke 6:31.)

The apostle Paul wrote a second letter to his servant Timothy warning him about life in the last days before Christ's return. Paul predicted that mankind would take a turn for the worse. Unfortunately, Paul was right on the money with his warning.

Our lives are not to reflect selfishness but kindness. To do this we must faithfully submit our selfish desires to the Holy Spirit. Submitting these desires won't be a cakewalk because our sinful nature is at war with the Spirit living within us. But we will honor God when we treat others the way we want to be treated. Who knows? Maybe someday someone will offer the last chocolate doughnut to you.

Weed and Water:

Being second or last in line isn't the end of the world. Someone has to be last. Think about Christ's words to his disciples, "The last will be first, and the first will be last" (Matthew 20:16) when you want to exalt your needs above the needs of others.

Sprout and Scatter:

Today be eager to let others go before you. At a four-way-stop sign, motion others to go first. Hold the elevator door and let everyone get off or on before you do. Don't take the closest parking space. Give up your spot in the checkout line. Play a game with your kids before you do what you want to do. Share the dessert you normally hoard with a member of your family. You'll brighten others' days as well as your own.

Think about it:

Whose needs come first in your household?

_____

_____

_____

_____

_____

Name three ways you are selfish:

_____

_____

_____

Prayer Pot:

Lord, forgive my selfishness and . . .

_____

_____

_____

_____

_____

Last-place finishers in the world's eyes
are first-place winners in God's eyes.

Kindness and Compassion

"The Lord is gracious and righteous; our God is full of compassion."

Psalm 116:5

Complete strangers reached out to the victims of the September 11th terrorist attacks with kindness and compassion. Whole communities shipped truckloads of goods to Ground Zero, including teddy bears for children who had lost parents or relatives. One charity gave teddy bears to surviving family members of Cantor Fitzgerald, the firm that lost all seven hundred of its employees on the top floors of the World Trade Towers.

Some days we all could use a teddy bear or bear hug, but stuffed teddies are only a temporary fix. A more lasting source of compassion comes from people demonstrating personal kindness to others. The Lord has placed his spirit of compassion within believers. Christ enables us to go out of our way to commiserate and be kind. Yet, as much as we try to help, sometimes we mess up. We say or do the wrong thing, or we don't do anything at all.

The best source of compassion and comfort is God. Today's seed reminds us that God understands our hurt and pain. Jesus

Dig Deeper:

"Compassion" as used in today's seed comes from the Hebrew word *racham*. We are to love deeply and to have mercy and tender affection for others.

was fully God, but also fully human, capable of all the emotions we experience. God can sympathize with us better than any human. He created us. He will never let us down. He understands our weaknesses. His kindness is genuine and everlasting.

Weed and Water:

Don't let yourself become the focus of the conversation when a hurting friend needs to talk. If you haven't experienced her troubles, you may find your compassion lacking. If you have never lost a child, you cannot understand the magnitude of that mother's sorrow. You may be tempted to judge. Ask God to fill you with his compassion so you can minister kindness to those who need it. Don't give unsolicited advice. Just be available and remember that healing comes slowly to some, quickly to others.

Sprout and Scatter:

Spend time listening to hurting people, and ask the Holy Spirit to speak sincere words of comfort through you. Your compassion can be active, too. Prepare meals, pick up a friend's child from soccer practice, or give a CD of soothing music. Offer to buy your friend a head covering if she looses her hair through chemotherapy. Visit the cemetery with a widow. Give lots of hugs! All of these ideas let kindness shine in tangible ways.

Think about it:

Name two reasons why God is the best source of compassion.

🐞 _____

🐞 _____

How will you show kindness to hurting people this week?

_____

_____

_____

_____

Prayer Pot:

Lord, let your kindness and compassion shine through me in . . .

_____

_____

_____

_____

_____

_____

"Little deeds of kindness, little words of love, Help to make earth happy like the heaven above."
—Julia A. Fletcher Carney, from "Little Things"

A Kindhearted Woman

Today's Seed

> "A kindhearted woman gains respect, but ruthless men gain only wealth."
>
> Proverbs 11:16

Respect is what every woman wants whether she is a grand-mother, aunt, sister, mother, or daughter. In the 1960s Aretha Franklin sang a song about getting R-E-S-P-E-C-T from a man. In doing so, she created quite a stir. Women claimed this tune as their own personal theme song because they no longer *wanted* respect; they demanded it.

In living the Christian life, a woman, regardless of her stature, must conduct herself in a manner that honors the Lord. This is our hope of gaining respect before men and God. Proverbs 31 describes a woman of noble character who was respected for her actions as a wife, mother, and manager of the home (just a few of her numerous mantles). Her husband says of her, "Give her the reward she has earned, and let her works bring her praise at the city gate" (Proverbs 31:31).

The Proverbs 31 woman was kindhearted. She got up before dawn to cook meals for her family and servants. She spent her

Dig Deeper:
Chrestos is used interchangeably with the word "gracious" to mean pleasant, good, and "kind" when speaking of a person's character.

days sewing clothes for her household and making coverings for their beds. She opened her arms to the poor and needy. (See Proverbs 31:20.) The woman was driven by kindness, and because of it she gained the respect of her husband and the people of their city. She didn't *demand* respect or try to gain it ruthlessly. She simply served people with a kind, gentle heart, as we are called to do.

Background Bulb:

There are dozens of godly women listed in the Bible. Deborah was a prophetess and the only female judge of Israel. Don't let the Proverbs 31 "ideal" woman intimidate you. Instead, study the qualities mentioned and allow the Holy Spirit to develop your character according to God's will for your life.

Weed and Water:

Are you considered a gracious friend, wife, or mother? Your gifts of kindness and tenderness may help to heal rifts in the world. Read Proverbs 31:10–31 and write down the traits, including kindness, that you see exhibited by the wife of noble character. Each day pick one of the traits and work on developing it in your own actions. Don't worry about gaining respect; if you live as God has called you to live, respect from others will be a by-product.

Think about it:

How can you gain respect before God and man?

_____

_____

_____

_____

List the three traits you value most, but possess the least from Proverbs 31.

_____

_____

_____

Prayer Pot:

O God, please help me develop into a woman who . . .

_____

_____

_____

_____

_____

_____

A little kindness goes a long way.

Why Kindness Is Not Enough

Today's Seed

"For it is by grace you have been saved, through faith—and this not from yourselves, it is the gift of God—not by works, so that no one can boast."

Ephesians 2:8–9

One local man's obituary read like a tribute to a modern-day saint. He attended church faithfully. He gave thousands of dollars to the public library and volunteered at the food pantry across town. Surely he entered heaven when he passed away and now keeps company with the angels.

Many kind souls have spent their lives spreading goodwill on the earth. However, some believers miss the mark by focusing on the deeds or works that they believe will grant them entrance into heaven. Or they believe that acts of kindness earn them brownie points with God. But today's seed reminds us that kind works are not enough. God will crown us with righteousness because of our good deeds, but He concerns himself mainly with the depth of our faith and our ability to trust Him for all we need.

Jesus refers to himself as the way, the truth, and the life. (See John 14:6.) It is our faith in Christ alone that saves us. Nowhere

Dig Deeper:

"Deeds" or "works" in the New Testament may be translated as the Greek word *ergon*, meaning to toil as an effort or occupation.

in the obituary was there a mention of the man's faith, other than his going to church once in a while. We must allow our deepening faith to lead us to good deeds rather than trusting our works to save us, for both are part of our testimony. Ultimately it is our faith that pleases God. And if our faith is strong, our deeds will be kind.

Background Bulb:

James 2:17 says, "In the same way, faith by itself, if it is not accompanied by action, is dead." Although we are saved by faith in Jesus Christ, good deeds are the way we show our faith to the world. Faith and works are inseparable. True faith produces good works of lasting value, repentance, and fruitfulness. Kind deeds alone get you nothing but a nice reputation.

Weed and Water:

Think about the words of advice you have given to people over the years. Make a mental list of the suggestions or admonitions you have offered to others. How do your own actions match up with your words? If you find you have been "talking the talk without walking the walk," seek God's forgiveness and attempt to back up your statements. Make a list of things you have said but not done, and do them.

Think about it:

Why is kindness (good works) less than adequate when it comes to the Christian life?

_____

_____

Does God view you as a person of faith or of kindness or both?

_____

_____

Spend a few moments examining your motives in doing good deeds.

_____

Prayer Pot:

Dear Lord, grant me the strength to live by faith and not by works, especially when I . . .

_____

_____

_____

_____

_____

Kindness is most effective when paired with faith.

Intentional Acts of Kindness

Today's Seed

"Therefore, as we have opportunity, let us do good to all people, especially those who belong to the family of believers."

Galatians 6:10

Jesus' ministry was full of random acts of kindness. At least that's how it seemed on the surface. Throngs of people followed the Lord from town to town seeking chance encounters with him. Many who followed him were probably entertained by the miracles Jesus performed. Others sought healing. It all looked spontaneous, but it wasn't.

For Jesus, ministry was intentional. One day he intentionally went through Samaria, an area Jews avoided, so that he could meet a needy woman on her way to a well at noon. This woman had a history—a bad history. The other women in town avoided her. But Jesus broke all the social rules and asked this woman to give him a drink of water from her pitcher. He talked with her and she ended up becoming a believer. (See John 4:4–30.) She even rounded up her whole town to see Jesus.

Dig Deeper:

Kairos is a Greek noun meaning a fixed and definite period, a time or season, and is translated "opportunity" in today's seed. Opportunities to practice kindness can be lost when we are focused on ourselves.

Jesus transformed lives because his purpose for being on earth was to minister to sick, sinful people in need of salvation. Everywhere he went and in everything he did, Jesus maintained a mentality of ministry. He even looked beyond people's physical needs and touched their souls, forgiving, cleansing, or rebuking. Jesus' life purpose enabled him to act with intentional kindness.

Our intentional acts can take many forms—bringing groceries to a family in need, giving to Christian ministries or missionaries, comforting those who grieve. Each day is the appropriate time to be kind to all people, especially those whom others may overlook.

Background Bulb:

"Divine appointment" is a phrase that has been around for generations. Although this phrase isn't found in the Bible, most God-fearing believers hold that he controls our circumstances. The world says that our path in life is one big roll of the dice. Believers recognize that God controls many opportunities in our lives, and we call these times divine appointments.

Sprout and Scatter:

Consider yourself a free agent for God. Ask God to lead you and empower you to be intentionally kind at least once a day. As you begin to pray and walk in the Spirit, you will discover opportunities unfolding. God will grant you divine appointments to plant seeds about him or reap a harvest by drawing others into the body of Christ. Consider starting a journal to record what God brings your way, what you do, and the results.

Think about it:

What sins might prevent a person from being kind?

_____

List two intentional acts of kindness that you can carry out this week.

_____

_____

What are some results that may come about from your kindness?

_____

_____

Prayer Pot:

Father, my kindness is nothing without your . . .

_____

_____

_____

_____

_____

_____

It's not enough to think about being kind; we must act on our intentions.

God's Bountiful Kindness

Today's Seed

> "Turn my eyes away from worthless things; preserve my life according to your word."
>
> Psalm 119:37

Fruit salad in the month of July or August is a special treat—watermelon chunks nestled next to ripe strawberries, blueberries, and maybe even raspberries. Yum! The flavors are succulent! Fresh fruit is good for our bodies because it provides vitamins A, C, and E—important nutrients. God designed our bodies to live on healthy foods. He also designed a way for our spiritual bodies to grow in strength and might. Our spiritual nourishment comes from his Word and the Holy Spirit.

God, in his bountiful kindness, gave us his written Word to carry with us in our daily lives. It is through the eternal goodness of God's Word that we learn about our Father's character and gain understanding of his kindness and mercy. Being saturated with God's Word is the beginning of aligning our lives with his character and spreading his kindness to others.

Imagine again a tasty fruit salad. When we spend time in the Word and in prayer, our spiritual fruit is healthy and full of life.

Dig Deeper:

"Preserve" or *chayah* as used in the Psalm has several meanings: to keep or make alive; to quicken or restore to life. God's Word is a preservative for our spiritual well-being.

Now imagine making fruit salad with fruit that is days old. Fruit flies take over and leave you with unrecognizable lumps. When we fail to read God's Word and focus instead on worthless things, aren't we more likely to be unkind and disobedient? We react to situations inappropriately because we have deprived our bodies of their spiritual nourishment.

God's Word does preserve us. It has the ability to keep us from worthless things and can keep our kindness from deteriorating. God can't use us when our fruit is moldy.

Background Bulb:

Psalm 119 is divided into twenty-two parts or stanzas, denoted by the twenty-two letters of the Hebrew alphabet. Verses 33–40 are devoted to the blessings of obeying God. The writer of this psalm asked God to literally turn his eyes away from worthless things. We need God's help to follow his decrees and to avoid being enticed or falling back into old behaviors.

Weed and Water:

Pray for the strength to resist pursuing worthless things. For some people coveting the biggest house on the block is a temptation. Others desire power, jewelry, success, or high-tech gadgets. When you find yourself desiring something without eternal value, open God's Word. It is filled with stories about different people who all discovered the same thing: only God is worth devoting your life to.

Think about it:

Is your life's fruit fresh or wilted from lack of nutrients and exposure to ungodliness?

_____

_____

How is God's Word relevant to you?

_____

_____

What worthy things will you now seek?

_____

_____

Prayer Pot:

Father, turn my eyes from worthless things and . . .

_____

_____

_____

_____

_____

_____

Fruit that is not used rots quickly.

He's Good

Today's Seed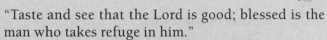

"Taste and see that the Lord is good; blessed is the man who takes refuge in him."

Psalm 34:8

Some of us may have the same habit children occasionally exhibit at the dinner table. We turn our noses up at unfamiliar food. We make a negative decision based on sight about something that can only be adequately judged by taste.

Unlike children, though, some of us continue to judge with one sense what only another sense can take in. We judge others with our eyes, determining by their look or skin color what type of person they are, when our ears, open to hear and understand, need to be the sense organ used in this case.

We have a tendency to judge the Lord with the wrong sense organs. We use our eyes to look at how church people act and we conclude that God is not for us when we see them do something we don't like. We use our ears to catch any hint of a slip of the tongue by a pastor and we decide to stop going to church. The truth is, God can only be experienced in our hearts. We have to taste him for ourselves. We have to see him for ourselves.

 Dig Deeper:

To "taste" is used figuratively here. It means to perceive, to become acquainted with by experience. To "see" means to inspect. Once we "taste" God this way, we learn he can be trusted and he becomes our refuge and hope.

Once we do experience him, we'll find that he is indeed ultimate goodness. And good tastes good!

Background Bulb:

If Thomas the disciple had been an American, he would have been from the Show Me state. In John 20:24–25, Thomas refused to believe that Jesus had risen from the dead unless he saw him with his own eyes and touched him with his own hands. Thomas needed a personal, sensory experience. When Jesus obliged, he gave those of us who weren't present a promise: "Because you [Thomas] have seen me, you have believed; blessed are those who have not seen and yet have believed."

Weed and Water:

Revel in the ultimate goodness of God simply because of who he is, not because of what he's done. Each day for the next twenty-six days, take a letter of the alphabet and write down words to express to God how good he is. For example, on Day 1, you could write, "God, you are awesome." On Day 2, write something like, "God, you are big and beautiful," and so on. Just adore him because of his goodness.

Think about it:

In what ways have you tasted or seen God's goodness?

_____

_____

_____

_____

What can you do to force yourself to recognize God's goodness on a daily basis?

_____

_____

_____

Prayer Pot:

Lord, thank you for your goodness in . . .

_____

_____

_____

_____

_____

_____

"To complain that man measures God by his own experience is a waste of time; he has no other yardstick."
—Dorothy L. Sayers

A Parent's Good Gifts

Today's Seed

"If you, then, though you are evil, know how to give good gifts to your children, how much more will your Father in heaven give good gifts to those who ask him!"

Matthew 7:11

During the holiday season, some toy stores stay open twenty-four hours. Why? Thousands of parents are seeking that perfect Christmas present for their children. It doesn't matter whether the child has been naughty or nice that year. Those parents wait in long lines and sometimes spend more than they planned just to see the excitement in those wide eyes on Christmas morning as children look under the tree. The children are not quite sure what they'll get but are confident that good old Mom or Dad will come through.

Today's seed emphasizes how we can relate to God as our parent—our Father—by recognizing the wonderful gifts he gives to us. He is even better at gift giving than we are. Parents aren't perfect. We sometimes give gifts that are not good for children in the long run. God, on the other hand, gives us good gifts out of his

Dig Deeper:
The Greek word for father (*pater*) means a nourisher, protector, and upholder.

perfection. He knows exactly what we need or should have—despite the things for which we beg.

As God's children, our needs for attention and provision are ongoing. We need God at all hours of the day and night. And just like on Christmas morning, we can approach God confidently, knowing that he always has good gifts for us as we look to the "Tree"—the Cross of Christ. There the greatest gift—the sacrifice of his Son—for our ultimate need, salvation, was given. And good Dads always supply good gifts for their children.

Background Bulb:

Today's seed is taken from a section of Scripture known as the Sermon on the Mount, the full text of which can be found in Matthew 5–7. All of this teaching is also known as the King's Manifesto. In other words, in this sermon given at the beginning of his earthly ministry, Jesus describes the attributes of his kingdom. This particular seed is part of a section instructing us on how to seek God's help.

Sprout and Scatter:

When we pray for our children, grandchildren, or other loved ones, we may think we know what they need. God, however, knows best. He wants us to confidently bring our requests to him just as we would ask things of a father we loved. But he also wants us to acknowledge that he knows what is best for our loved ones. He wants us to relax, trusting God that he always gives good gifts because he is a perfect Father who looks out for others' long-term good.

Think about it:

What gift have you gone out of your way to buy or make?

_____

_____

Imagine God doing the same thing for you. How does that make you feel?

_____

_____

What have you failed to ask God for because you forgot he is a perfect Father?

_____

_____

Prayer Pot:

Lord, be my perfect Father. Thanks for giving me . . .

_____

_____

_____

_____

_____

"Becoming a father is easy enough,
But being one can be rough."
—Wilhelm Busch, _Julchen_, 1877

Seeing Goodness in Hard Times

Today's Seed

> "I am still confident of this: I will see the goodness of the Lord in the land of the living."
>
> Psalm 27:13

Corrie ten Boom watched as the man she loved proposed to and married another woman. Corrie never married.

Ann's house burned to the ground not once but three times.

Tina's son committed suicide.

In Psalm 27 David, who wrote today's seed, mentions some of his problems—"small" things like armies and wars arising against him, people lying about him, worries about his parents rejecting him. But David didn't despair. He prayed and asked God to hear his cries for help and to be merciful to him. From there David rebounded. Even through his most difficult struggles, David chose to maintain faith in God's goodness.

God promises not to put us through more than we can handle. We may experience more than we can handle *alone*, but through him all things are possible. Learning to be totally reliant on God to get through tough times is the reason for the hardships. It is then that we are willing to allow God's goodness of grace, love,

Dig Deeper:

Goodness is defined as moral excellence and praiseworthy character. God's goodness is seen in such attributes as kindness, grace, love, and righteousness.

and righteousness to be most active in our lives. This is a very *good* thing.

৬ Weed and Water:

The next time you face a hard time, deliberately look for the blessing in it. For example, when a child comes home after curfew, praise God that he did indeed come home. When you're passed over for a promotion, thank God you weren't laid off. When you argue with your spouse, be grateful that you have someone who cares enough about you to try to get you to understand his point.

Sprout and Scatter:

Help children see God's goodness by praying with them about their desires. Instead of immediately agreeing to their requests for toys or trips to an amusement park, tell them, "Let's pray about that and ask God if he wants you to have the toy (or go on the trip)." If the answer is "yes," thank the Lord with the children. If the answer is "wait" because of lack of money, allow the children to watch you trust God for the provision. If the answer is "no," thank God for his guidance. Ask God to help them gain understanding through their disappointment.

Think about it:

How has God been good to you today?

_____

_____

_____

What is one good thing you can see in your current hard time?

_____

_____

_____

Prayer Pot:

Thank you, Lord, for your goodness today in the area(s) of . . .

_____

_____

_____

_____

_____

_____

_____

"Surely goodness and love will follow
me all the days of my life, and I will
dwell in the house of the Lord forever."
—Psalm 23:6

Praise God's Goodness

"They will celebrate your abundant goodness and
joyfully sing of your righteousness."
Psalm 145:7

People of different denominations express their praise to God in
different ways when they worship. One congregation worships by
kneeling for prayer, standing to sing, and sitting to listen to the
sermon. Another group worships by listening quietly to the choir
and the pastor's sermon. Still other congregations worship with
corporate singing and clapping and by shouting "Amen" and
"Praise the Lord" as the pastor preaches.

No matter the manner, the point is the same—to praise God.
Praise is an expression of favorable judgment. We can praise God
and be seen by others, or we can praise God through quiet prayer
and be seen by no one. Reflecting upon God's goodness is enough
to elicit whatever kind of praise we're comfortable givings
whether it's a smile and a nod or a raised hand and teary eyes.

Along with our regular way of worship, it's also a good idea to
try to celebrate God's goodness in new ways. Just like it's fun to

Dig Deeper:
"Celebrate" in this seed can also be translated "abun-
dantly utter" or "pour out." Let your praise of God pour
out.

try a new recipe or a new food so it's fun to "taste" new ways of praising God.

Background Bulb:

In 2 Samuel 6:14, King David was so happy about the return of the ark of the covenant to the people of Israel that he danced before the Lord with all his might. His wife Michal was embarrassed by her husband's unbridled expression. She thought David didn't look dignified or kingly as he danced in the streets. She worried about what others thought. However, David rebuked his wife because she didn't understand that outward praise of God's goodness is for an audience of one—God—and is always acceptable.

Weed and Water:

The Bible tells of many methods and postures for praising God. Our praise can be expressed through song, prayer, and testimony. We can stand, kneel, or lie on our faces. We can clap or lift our hands. According to Psalm 150, we can even use all kinds of musical instruments. Expand your praise. Try praising God in a different manner and in a different posture from your usual stance.

Think about it:

What is your usual manner and posture when praising God?

_____

_____

What manner and posture will you try?

_____

_____

After you've tried this new praise method, note here how you felt.

_____

_____

Prayer Pot:

Lord, I praise you for your goodness in . . .

_____

_____

_____

_____

_____

_____

Praise is the vehicle we use to express our appreciation to the Lord and our excitement and thanks for all he is and has done.

Good Versus Evil

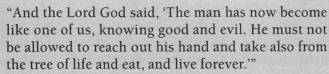

Today's Seed

"And the Lord God said, 'The man has now become like one of us, knowing good and evil. He must not be allowed to reach out his hand and take also from the tree of life and eat, and live forever.'"

Genesis 3:22

No one can dispute that injustice, hurt, and wickedness abound in our world. Even criminals who are caught in the act of their crimes and who plead "not guilty" attempt to justify their actions by saying they weren't responsible. Their very attempt to excuse their behavior shows that they know good from evil.

Likewise, we are quick to feel incensed when we've been treated unjustly because we have an inborn sense of right and wrong. Worse yet, because of the fall, we have intimate experiences with unpleasant thoughts, painful feelings, gossip, betrayal, grief, and death.

Adam and Eve's punishment for eating the forbidden fruit was death. The moment they ate, their innocence died. Their happiness withered. Their dreams vanished. Oh, the heartache that they suddenly felt! They hadn't considered that it might be better for them not to know or experience evil. Until they ate of the forbidden fruit,

Dig Deeper:
Evil is the upheaval of divine harmony. Moral evil involves a person's refusal to obey God's will.

they had experienced only goodness. They knew about evil only in an academic sense—in the sense of understanding the rules they needed to obey. Once they disobeyed, they and all people afterward have the "pleasure" of experiencing and doing evil.

The physical death that began on that day is actually a blessing from God's goodness. He relieved us from having to live forever in this world of struggle and heartache. In his goodness he provided a way of escape for us through his Son, Jesus. Our connection to God through the Holy Spirit enables us to identify, attack, or shun evil when it comes our way.

Background Bulb:

God, being perfect, understands evil. By personal experience, though, he knows only good. It was God's goodness that shielded Adam and Eve from knowing evil before they chose to disobey God. When they disobeyed, all creation suffered. A woman's freedom as coruler with her husband died. Freedom from pain in childbirth died and ultimately physical death began. The sin of Adam and Eve extended to all of nature too. The ground became unruly and uncooperative by bringing forth thorns. Work, originally meant to be rewarding, now became drudgery because of evil.

Weed and Water:

Prayer and consistent exposure to the Word of God will build discernment, which is the ability to make wise choices. The more time we spend in God's Word, the more sensitive we become to the Holy Spirit's leading. The next time you face a choice, ask God to reveal his will to you. Then find Scripture to support the choice you are thinking of making.

Think about it:

What was the last evil thing, poor choice, or wrong action you committed?

_____

_____

How could you have avoided it?

_____

_____

What will you do to avoid wrong action in the future?

_____

_____

Prayer Pot:

Lord, show me the difference between good and evil in my choices about . . .

_____

_____

_____

_____

_____

"Of two evils, choose neither."
—Charles H. Spurgeon

Goodness Seen in Unity

Today's Seed

> "How good and pleasant it is when brothers live together in unity!"
>
> Psalm 133:1

Peace is so much more pleasant than discord. No one is happy when there's turmoil. Yet, we allow the littlest things to rock our boats. For example, a brunette teenager makes the decision to dye his hair blonde or pierce his ear. If one parent disapproves, this incident can snowball into a major family feud. A bride may want a small, intimate wedding, but her parents want to invite everyone they've ever known. They can get into such an argument that the couple elopes and no one has the wedding experience.

Church families are not exempt from feuds. Congregations have split over silly issues like who leads the choir and the type of music they sing.

For the sake of unity sometimes we must give up our "rights" and stop campaigning for the way we think things should be run. We submit to God by seeking unity and allowing the other person to have her way as long as that way is not in direct opposition to Scripture. Goodness is seen through unity, whether it is family or church unity.

Dig Deeper:
Unity has to do with harmony and agreement, a oneness of purpose and behavior among the people of God.

A popular church song says, "They'll know we are Christians by our love." All Christians should be people who live in unity with one another. To do otherwise would be detrimental to our witness.

Background Bulb:

Unity gets things done both positively and negatively. In the case of the tower of Babel as recorded in Genesis 11, the people were unified and decided to build a tower that would reach to heaven so that they would not have to be scattered over the earth. Because they had a unified purpose, they were being successful. The only problem was they weren't supposed to stay together. God had told them to replenish the earth, to move, and scatter. Even though their purpose was against God, they were getting it done because they were unified. God had to thwart their plan.

Sprout and Scatter:

Name this month as home-unity month. Have each family member name a project and claim a week as his or her own. For example, clean the garage for Dad one week, and install a basketball pole for Junior the next. During the week have all other family members promote goodness through unity by working with that family member on his or her project. You will be surprised at the amount of work that gets done and the fun you have doing it. This exercise can work with churches or auxiliaries as well.

Think about it:

Describe the last time you worked on a successful team.

_____

_____

What is someone you know doing alone that could be done better through your unified efforts?

_____

_____

How and when will you get involved?

_____

_____

Prayer Pot:

Lord, help me to promote unity by . . .

_____

_____

_____

_____

_____

_____

"In necessary things, unity; in doubtful things, liberty; in all things, charity."
—Richard Baxter

Thanks, I Needed That

*Today's
Seed*

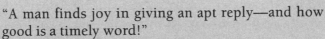

"A man finds joy in giving an apt reply—and how good is a timely word!"

Proverbs 15:23

You're asked to be the chairperson of this year's charity fashion show. You're excited. In fact, you consider it an honor because this is an important event for your community. You realize it will take hard work and determination, but you have great people working on the committee with you so you have no doubt you can pull it off.

As the event gets closer, however, the pressure and the demands increase. You're swamped. You begin to feel like it will be impossible to have everything finished in time. Your patience is short. Your temper is on edge. Then the phone rings.

Your first reaction is, "What now?" but you quell that thought and answer the phone. A committee member's voice on the other end says, "I just called to say you are doing a magnificent job planning the fashion show. Your organization and gentle spirit are helping the rest of us work as a team. Have a good day."

Although you hang up the phone in shock, you are smiling.

Dig Deeper:

The word "timely" in today's seed is rendered "in due season" in another Bible version. Both renderings mean that something is to be done at its most appropriate moment.

That word of encouragement was just what you needed to hear. You are calmed and refreshed, ready to face the challenges ahead.

A word of encouragement recharges and rejuvenates. Show goodness by speaking encouraging words. The joy will bounce right back to you when the person will most likely respond, "Thanks, that's just what I needed to hear."

Weed and Water:

A word aptly spoken may mean giving advice. Before you offer advice, though, discern if your help would be considered timely. Use this acrostic to THINK before you speak by asking yourself these questions: Is what I want to say True? Is it Honest? Is it Important? Is it Necessary? Is it Kind? If the answer is "no" to any of these questions, don't share the information.

Sprout and Scatter:

This month speak a kind word to someone every day. Tell a family member how much you appreciate his or her cooking. Call an old friend and reminisce about a happy time, letting her know it wouldn't have been the same without her. Compliment a stranger on how nice she looks in her suit. By the end of thirty days, you will have probably developed the habit of giving encouraging words and you'll feel better because you will have smiled much more that month.

Think about it:

List two people who need to hear some positive words.

_____

_____

What will you say to them, and when will you say it?

_____

_____

Prayer Pot:

Lord, speak your words through my lips . . .

_____

_____

_____

_____

_____

_____

_____

"[Like] apples of gold in settings of silver is a word spoken in right circumstances."
—Proverbs 25:11 NAS

Let It Grow

"Through these [God's glory and goodness] he has given us his very great and precious promises, so that through them you may participate in the divine nature and escape the corruption in the world caused by evil desires. For this very reason, make every effort to add to your faith goodness; and to goodness, knowledge;"

2 Peter 1:4–5

There are habits, skills, and virtues that everyone would do well to master. Good hygiene and proper eating habits help us stay healthy. Reading and writing are skills that enable us to communicate effectively. Courtesy and respect are virtues that enable us to get along happily with our fellow humans.

In each case, cultivating these traits happens over time. As children we learn the abc's and how to craft a good sentence. By the time we become adults, we can write a paragraph to thank someone and, hopefully, can understand some of the fine print in our insurance policies. As toddlers we learn to say "please" and "thank you," and, hopefully, as adults we become courteous and thoughtful of others.

Dig Deeper:

In New Testament times the word "add" was used to mean lavish or abundant provision. God doesn't want us to do the bare minimum. He wants us to be rich in goodness and knowledge.

The more we work at something the better at it we become. We don't just wake up one day with instant understanding of legal jargon—as much as we might wish that would happen. It is our responsibility to expend effort to cultivate and sharpen our skills in the areas in which we wish to excel. Two traits that should be on our to-do lists are goodness and knowledge.

By faith in Christ we receive salvation and along with it we receive the "precious promises" referred to in today's seed—his divine nature and the ability to cultivate Christlikeness. God does not tell us to do what is impossible; he equips us for the job. Neither do we suddenly act consistently good. We must work at it. It takes practice.

Weed and Water:

With zeal and seriousness of purpose we are to pursue the holiness that characterizes the Christian life. Goodness is moral excellence that translates into happiness and wise living. Knowledge refers to knowing God's will, which leads to obedient living. Each virtue is like a stair on a staircase, building one on top of the other and bringing us closer to God. Are you climbing those stairs with zeal and seriousness?

Sprout and Scatter:

Be creative in cultivating goodness. As you are using your faith to trust God to develop goodness in you, embrace the process by doing things for others. Every now and then, as you see someone doing a good deed, join in. Two heads are better than one and four hands work faster than two. Help a friend make her goodness even better.

Think about it:

On a scale of one to five how well have you added goodness to your faith?

_____

_____

_____

How can you be more lavish in your quest for goodness and knowledge?

_____

_____

_____

Prayer Pot:

Lord, show me how to develop goodness in . . .

_____

_____

_____

_____

_____

"Goodness is love in action with its hand to the plow."
—James Hamilton

I See It

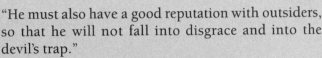

*Today's
Seed*

"He must also have a good reputation with outsiders, so that he will not fall into disgrace and into the devil's trap."

1 Timothy 3:7

An adult Sunday school teacher was respected in his church. Outside of the church family, however, he was known to be slow at paying his bills. Although he lived in a beautiful home, drove an expensive car, and treated family and friends to dinner at first-rate restaurants, he pleaded forgetfulness or lack of money when painters or plumbers called about overdue bills. His poor reputation among blue-collar workers caused them to grumble about his Christianity.

Christians are role models. As soon as folks discover our dedication to the Lord, they watch us. How do we react to a gas crisis, rising taxes, the upcoming election, and the different-race family who moves in next door? How do we cope with a rebellious teenager, a financial reversal, or a death in our family?

Having a good reputation among our neighbors means we live in such a way that they see something admirable in our lives.

Dig Deeper:

The word "trap" comes from a Greek word that carries with it the idea of being held by a noose. The devil's traps are tricks and temptations, skillfully designed to choke the very life out of us.

Realizing that others are looking up to us and are evaluating Christianity based on our actions helps to keep us from wandering into the traps of the devil.

As others watch us, we want them to be drawn toward relationship with God, not away from it.

Background Bulb:

Today's seed was advice given to Timothy, a young minister, by Paul, the seasoned church planter. Not only was Timothy young but also he was probably younger than those to whom he ministered. In 1 and 2 Timothy, Paul gives this young man practical wisdom about how to live before others so as to gain their respect and not shame the name of Christ. Today's seed is part of fifteen qualifications Paul told Timothy to look for in choosing godly church leaders.

Weed and Water:

Examine your small actions about which you've never thought in a spiritual way. Do you pay your bills on time? Do you treat blue-collar workers with respect? Do you roll your eyes when frustrated? Do you cross your arms when you're tired of listening to someone talk? Do you put off returning phone calls that you know may be important to the other party? Ask yourself and God if these little gestures and small habits are contributing to your having a good or bad reputation in the eyes of others.

Think about it:

What in my lifestyle would receive a good report from my neighbors and coworkers?

_____

_____

What in my life would detract from my good reputation?

_____

_____

How can I become aware of any other bad habits?

_____

_____

Prayer Pot:

Lord, open my eyes to my sin and forgive me for . . .

_____

_____

_____

_____

_____

_____

"He that is good for making excuses is seldom good for anything else."
—Benjamin Franklin

Experienced in Goodness

Today's Seed

> "I myself am convinced, my brothers, that you your-
> selves are full of goodness, complete in knowledge
> and competent to instruct one another."
>
> Romans 15:14

Speed kills. Although teens want to be good drivers, they often
drive too fast. They don't know that the wet roadway around the
curve ahead is slick. They don't think *they* will be in an accident.
Adults have experienced the unexpected and know to plan for
such possibilities. They usually drive more slowly and urge their
teens to do the same. Age has a few advantages—although taut
skin and rock-hard muscles may not be among them.

Today's seed is the second one that has linked goodness to
knowledge. The first seed we studied was 2 Peter 1:4–5. Why is
knowledge necessary for goodness? Desiring to do the right thing
is great, but sometimes we don't know what to do or not do.
Knowledge of Scripture informs our actions, helping us to be full
of goodness.

Experience with life's hard knocks and God's provision and
care also bring with them a maturity that enables us to counsel

Dig Deeper:

The word "knowledge" in this seed and in 2 Peter 1:5
doesn't mean IQ. It means knowledge that enables you
to avoid mistakes and sins. It's a knowledge that's always
growing

others. We don't have to do something bad to know it's wrong. But after we suffer consequences from sin, we are more likely to urge others: "Don't do as I did. I want to spare you my pain."

Since they were experienced in faith, goodness, and knowledge, Paul wanted the Romans to instruct each other. They had firm faith in God, knowledge of his Word, and the ability to act on that knowledge. We can all take a lesson from that.

Background Bulb:

In Romans 1:7–8 Paul commends his readers because their "faith is being reported all over the world." Despite the persecution they suffered, Paul was excited that the Christians in Rome had a good reputation, such a good reputation that everywhere he went (and he traveled a lot), he heard of their Christian witness. Now they were ready to pass that goodness on to others. They stayed strong—strong enough to receive a commendation from Paul and strong enough to be examples for us.

Sprout and Scatter:

Give your friends or children yellow tickets for one month whenever they exhibit the virtue of goodness. Tell them to keep those tickets in a safe place, but don't tell them why. At the end of the month, ask them to bring their tickets to you. Collect them and treat those friends or your kids to a dinner in honor of their goodness. Tell them that their goodness "paid off." You will help them learn through experience that goodness is worthwhile.

Think about it:

If you were paid $10 for every act of goodness and charged $10 for every negative act, would you be in the black or in the red by the end of the month? (PMS days don't count!)

_____

_____

What can you do to instruct others from your well of goodness and knowledge?

_____

_____

_____

Prayer Pot:

Lord, grant that I may pass my goodness and knowledge to others by . . .

_____

_____

_____

_____

"Experience is the best of schoolmasters, only the school fees are heavy."
—Thomas Carlyle

Faithful Promise Keeper

Today's Seed

> "He remembers his covenant forever, the word he commanded, for a thousand generations."
>
> Psalm 105:8

"But, Mommy, you promised!"

Ever heard that whine? It is usually uttered when a child is desperate to get her own way. Good parenting includes keeping promises, but even the best of us sometimes fail to do what we said we would do.

Not so with God. He is the ultimate promise keeper. Throughout the Bible he has made covenants with his people and he has never failed. He promised Noah that he would never destroy the earth with a flood again and gave the rainbow to remind us. He promised Abraham, Isaac, and Jacob that their descendants would live in the Promised Land. Then he brought Moses on the scene to take them there.

God's most important promise was the promise of a Messiah—the Savior of all. Jesus Christ is the fulfillment of that promise. God promises that Jesus will one day come again and rule the earth. It doesn't matter how many years go by, we can look for Jesus to come because God is a promise keeper.

Dig Deeper:

"Forever" is never ending. It means continuous past and infinite future. There is no time limit on God's promises.

Following God's example, we can become promise keepers too. But it means we have to develop a strong commitment to our word. Jesus kept his promise until it hurt. In the Garden of Gethsemane he realized the pain facing him, yet he said, "Your will be done" (Matthew 26:42). Then his promises held him on the cross. He could have summoned angels to rescue him, but he was faithful to God's salvation plan.

Weed and Water:

Promise keeping is a matter of integrity and diligence. James taught that we don't need superstition or platitudes to invoke promise-keeping character. "Above all, my brothers, do not swear—not by heaven or by earth or by anything else. Let your 'yes' be yes, and your 'no,' no, or you will be condemned" (James 5:12). Forget knocking on wood or holding a rabbit's foot or invoking Girl Scouts' honor. Build your reputation on honesty and integrity.

Sprout and Scatter:

As you turn down fun invitations in order to honor prior commitments, be they to your children or your employer, don't think that no one notices. You can inspire and encourage others to keep their promises as you keep yours. As the saying goes: values are more often caught than taught.

Think about it:

List some promises that you have made and kept.

_____

_____

_____

List some promises that you can make to your family.

_____

_____

_____

Prayer Pot:

Lord, help me be a faithful promise keeper when I . . .

_____

_____

_____

_____

_____

_____

_____

"Rest on God's promises; stand behind yours."
　　　　—Bruce and Stan

Creation Teaches Faithfulness

Today's Seed

> "For great is your love, reaching to the heavens; your faithfulness reaches to the skies."
>
> Psalm 57:10

In Texas cattle fields, small white birds linger beside cows while they feed on the green grass. As the cow pulls up a clump of grass, the bird quickly grabs the grasshoppers and other insects.

In the waters of the Caribbean, a large fish hovers in a rocky place while tiny fish like miniature mechanics remove parasites from its scales. The diminutive hummingbird hitches a ride on the back of geese flying south for the winter.

Conventional wisdom would have us believe that these creatures just happened to evolve in a way that they take care of each other. But the Bible reveals that God, the Creator, made provision for all creatures great and small. Only a God of great wisdom could be so creative. Only a God of great faithfulness would take care of the smallest details.

Jesus said that the Father knows and cares about everything in our lives. Just as he cares for tiny lizards who turn brown on brown surfaces and green on green surfaces, he cares whether you

Dig Deeper:

The word "faithfulness" comes from the Hebrew word *emeth*. It is a portrait of reliability, stability, and truth. God is the perfect picture of faithfulness.

get your work done and whether you find a parking place at the market. He is faithful to watch over every detail.

Background Bulb:

God is faithful no matter how men act. He clothed Adam and Eve though they disobeyed. He rescued rebellious Israel time and time again. He restored Peter to full service and ministry even though Peter had denied him three times. He is always faithful to you as well. When you disobey, he still loves you. When you fail to love and forgive, he gently reminds you. When the winds of disobedience and rebellion blow through your life, he is stable, loving, and faithful. His faithfulness is as big as the sky. No matter what the weather, he doesn't change.

Sprout and Scatter:

We can praise God for who he is and praise him for what he has done. To adore him for who he is, repeat statements about his character, greatness, love, mercy, and faithfulness, using examples from Psalms: "Lord God Almighty, who is like you? You are mighty, O Lord, and your faithfulness surrounds you" (Psalm 89:8). To adore him for what he has done, look around. Recite the blessings you see: your health, home, family, church, and friends. Practice these two techniques in private prayer and with a friend. God's faithfulness is worthy of our praise.

Think about it:

What amazing thing have you noticed about God's creation?

_____

_____

_____

How does nature inspire you to be more faithful?

_____

_____

_____

_____

Prayer Pot:

Lord, thank you for your faithfulness in all creation, especially . . .

_____

_____

_____

_____

_____

"His eye is on the sparrow and I know he watches me."
—Civilla D. Martin

The Root of Confidence

Today's Seed

"Such confidence as this is ours through Christ before God. Not that we are competent in ourselves to claim anything for ourselves, but our competence comes from God."

2 Corinthians 3:4–5

Everywhere you look—magazines, radio, television—there are courses, approaches, and suggestions on how to gain confidence. The how-to bookshelves are filled with ways to become confident and capable. The majority of these books and our popular media tell us to reach down deep inside ourselves and pull up the power to be a success. Confidence, they say, comes from inside.

Confidence is an important element in our lives and we need that sense of ability, but true confidence doesn't come from deep inside us. It comes from God. We have confidence because we understand that God is faithful. He never varies and he never fails.

Paul traced his success to God. He knew that God authored his confidence. Paul had a lot to brag about personally. In Philippians 3, we can read about his pedigreed ancestry, his record of excellent work, his amazing activities for the Lord, and his blameless

Dig Deeper:

The Greek word translated "claim" is *logizomal*. It means to count. When we count our abilities without God, our result is zero.

life of morality. Yet Paul did not take credit for any of his successes. He knew that God's faithfulness was the reason for all the good things in his life.

Speed records in racing, high scores in games, and innovative technical advances in computers are impressive, but nothing is truly worthwhile unless God is the one directing it all.

Background Bulb:

Today's seed is part of a letter Paul wrote to the church in Corinth. Earlier in the letter he wrote about his success in ministry. He was not bragging. He didn't need praise from others or letters of recommendation to commend him to people he didn't know because the people in the church were living proof of his message. Corinth was a wicked city, but many Corinthians had become Christians and through God's power were changing their behavior. Paul told them they were his testimonial letters (2 Corinthians 3:2).

Sprout and Scatter:

Can we have the kind of impact that Paul had? According to verse 4, we can through Jesus Christ. If we want to help others like Paul did, we must learn what Paul learned: competence comes from God. If you are confident despite obstacles and setbacks, people will see that you are relying on a faithful God. They will want to know how they can find the same kind of confidence.

Think about it:

What have you tried as your formula for success?

_____

_____

_____

_____

How can you make God's faithfulness your source for confidence?

_____

_____

_____

_____

_____

Prayer Pot:

Lord, thank you for your faithfulness concerning . . .

_____

_____

_____

_____

Every success is traced to God. Every hope is dependent on him.

The Faithfulness of Jesus

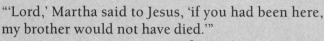

Today's Seed

> "'Lord,' Martha said to Jesus, 'if you had been here, my brother would not have died.'"
>
> John 11:21

Martha was angry. Though she had tried every remedy she knew, nothing worked. She had always been a woman who could get things done, sometimes by shear bent of personality. This time she lost the battle. Now her beloved brother, Lazarus, was dead. The anger boiling inside of her spilled out when Jesus finally arrived and she said the words in today's seed. Amazingly, Jesus did not rebuke her.

A few minutes later when Martha's sister, Mary, saw Jesus, she said the same words: "If you had been here, my brother would not have died." However Mary's personality was different from Martha's. Mary was quieter and more contemplative than Martha. Her words to Jesus, though the same, were uttered more in grief and resignation than in anger.

The words of the two sisters help us understand that we can come to Jesus with our problems because he is faithful to hear and answer us. We can express any emotion to him—even anger,

Dig Deeper:

When Martha called Jesus, "Lord," she used the Greek word *kurios*, which means supreme authority. Even in her grief, she recognized that Jesus was God in charge of the universe.

disappointment, denial, and grief. He is never surprised or shocked by our outbursts.

If we reveal our fears in times of illness, God is not upset with us. If we lose control, he is not shocked or overwhelmed. If we panic, he is not stunned. His faithfulness rises above our personalities and our petty problems.

Background Bulb:

Martha, Mary, and Lazarus were friends of Jesus. He often came to their house. Scholars believe that their home was a refuge for him, a place where he could relax and retreat from the pressures of the crowds that followed him. Since they had a personal relationship with Jesus and had contact with him often, Martha and Mary felt the freedom to speak their minds to him. Our ability to "tell Jesus" is directly related to how much time we spend with him and how well we know him.

Weed and Water:

Jesus' calm reaction to Martha's angry words and Mary's brooding words helps us see that he understands our emotions. He doesn't condemn us for getting angry or give up on us when we shout, "Why, Lord? Why?" He knows that we must face our hurts before we can fall into his arms of love. Our challenge is to be sure that we do not stay angry at God. After we have had our pity party or temper tantrum, we must accept the embrace of Jesus.

Think about it:

What event in your life has caused you to question God's faithfulness?

_____

_____

_____

What do you need to do to turn from your anger and doubts to embrace Jesus?

_____

_____

_____

_____

Prayer Pot:

Lord, forgive my pity parties and temper tantrums. Help me . . .

_____

_____

_____

_____

_____

_____

God never tires of hearing from us.

Faithful to Pray

Today's Seed

> "As for me, far be it from me that I should sin against the Lord by failing to pray for you."
>
> 1 Samuel 12:23a

One friend is a devoted Christian, but her husband has no interest in spiritual things. Another friend cares for her invalid mother with no help from her siblings. Another friend's child is chronically ill. Another struggles with depression. Our lists of cares and needs go on and on. The question is have we prayed?

Sometimes when we have tried everything—talking, begging, explaining, helping—we think there is nothing left to do but pray. But prayer is not the last resort. It is not simply one thing we haven't tried yet. Prayer is the best thing we can do. Prayer is the first place we should go.

It is the place we must return to over and over. Our fix-it mentality tries to come up with solutions and ten steps to recovery, but the Bible says, "Cast all your anxiety on him because he cares for you" (1 Peter 5:7).

Jesus understood the importance of faithful prayer. He prayed continually. He often went to a mountain or solitary place to pray.

Dig Deeper:

"Failing" is translated from the Hebrew word *chadal*. It comes from the root word "flabby." Not being faithful in prayer makes us soft, weak, and out of shape.

He placed his hands on children and prayed for them (Matthew 19:13). He taught his disciples to pray (Matthew 6:9–13). He told us to pray for everything and everyone—our enemies too (Luke 6:28). Jesus even prayed for us: "My prayer is not for them [the disciples] alone. I pray also for those who will believe [that's us!] in me through their message" (John 17:20–21).

Background Bulb:

Today's seed is part of Samuel's farewell speech. Samuel was a mighty prophet of Israel. He spoke the Word of God to the nation and taught God's Word for living. Israel, however, had been rebellious and wicked. In Samuel's last sermon, he listed the evidence. Israel had forgotten that God was their king and asked instead for a man to be their king. God provided Saul as king, but he was a miserable failure. The people were afraid. Samuel promised to faithfully pray for them.

Sprout and Scatter:

Here's a way to be faithful in prayer. Record all prayer requests in a purse-sized notepad or journal. When you are waiting in line or at a traffic light, open the notebook and pray. Start an e-mail loop with several friends and write prayers to each other. When someone asks you to pray, do it immediately—right there on the phone or in the store.

Think about it:

What does it mean to you to know that Jesus prayed for you?

_____

_____

How does faithful prayer help a friend's situation?

_____

_____

What will you do to become more faithful in prayer?

_____

_____

Prayer Pot:

Lord, help me remember to pray first and faithfully about . . .

_____

_____

_____

_____

_____

_____

A real friend warms you by her presence, trusts you with her secrets, and remembers you in her prayers.
—Anonymous

Faithfully Clinging

*Today's
Seed*

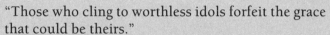

"Those who cling to worthless idols forfeit the grace that could be theirs."

Jonah 2:8

Is there an outfit in your closet that you have not worn in the past year? Perhaps you intended to wear it but you never got that button sewn on or lost those extra pounds. You own the garment but it has no value in its current condition.

We can't seem to let go of things even if they have no value. Modern society clings to homes, bank accounts, and exotic vacations, but these things are as worthless as the idols of Jonah's day.

People in Jonah's day followed foolish superstitions and fears as they worshiped gods of rock and wood. We follow dreams of fame and fortune, which can never bring us true happiness. Unless what we faithfully cling to is God, we are holding on to thin air.

According to today's seed, we "forfeit the grace" that could have been ours if we cling to the wrong things. Grace is the undeserved favor of God. He looked at us in mercy and extended his hand of grace to us. All he asks from us is that we are faithful to

Dig Deeper:

The Hebrew word for worthless is *shav*. It means emptiness and nothingness. Eventually each one of us faces a void after we have obtained possessions and fame.

ask him for all our needs. Giving up the favor and encouragement of God for the accumulation of things that are ultimately worthless isn't a good trade.

Background Bulb:

Today's seed is part of Jonah's prayer when he was inside the great fish. His prayer is recognition of his own rebellion when he disobeyed God and refused to go to Nineveh. Jonah was clinging to his prejudices and hatred for the Ninevites instead of his love for God. Holding on to these worthless attitudes caused him to disobey God and got him into a lot of trouble. In his prayer he is now clinging to God. Everything he held dear has been stripped away.

Weed and Water:

Clean the closet of your heart and make sure you are not clinging to worthless things. Examine yourself. Do you secretly put your hopes in financial security? Are you more concerned about how much you possess than about who possesses you? Are you living in your own strength rather than putting your trust in God? Do you believe that you can be successful because of your own abilities? God is ready to pour his grace on your life when you are ready to cling to him.

Think about it:

What possessions give you a feeling of security?

_____

_____

Are you faithful to trust God for the future? How?

_____

_____

How can you be more faithful to cling to God?

_____

_____

_____

Prayer Pot:

Lord, help me faithfully cling to you for . . .

_____

_____

_____

_____

_____

_____

Stick with God. He's the superglue
that holds the world together.

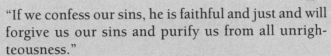

Faithful Light

Today's Seed

> "If we confess our sins, he is faithful and just and will forgive us our sins and purify us from all unrighteousness."
>
> 1 John 1:9

An electrical outage caused by Hurricane Alicia brought total darkness to the city. No lights in the homes or shops. No streetlights. No visible moon. The thick darkness proved the old saying, "You couldn't see your hand before your face."

Flashlights were helpful but merely illuminated a small circle. Only the morning sunlight brought relief from the darkness.

Sometimes we don't realize the darkness and blackness that cover our Christian walk. It is as if our heart has many compartments. We often hide bad attitudes and wrong actions in the unlighted rooms and darkest corners. We believe if we don't think about them, they'll go away. We don't want our friends to see jealousy or anger, so we hide it hoping no one will know.

We think we have hidden the sin from God too, but our faithful heavenly father's light reveals the darkest places in our hearts. Before we can ask for forgiveness, we have to know that we have sinned. That's the job of God's light. He shines his spotlight into

Dig Deeper:

The word "confess" comes from the Greek word *homologeo*, meaning to agree with. God already knows our faults, failures, and sins. He turns on the lights so we can see them too.

the corners and reveals the thing we tried to hide. His light is completely faithful. It never fails. "This is the message we have heard from him and declare to you: God is light; in him there is no darkness at all" (1 John 1:5).

Weed and Water:

When the Lord rescued us from darkness, he gave us a desire to live a holy and pure life. None of us wants to harbor dark sins in our hearts. On the other hand, it is not pleasant to clean out our spiritual closets. Don't let your secret sins stay secret. Drag them to the light of God. Let him look them over. Allow him to become the light of your life. He is the faithful light that forgives and removes sin.

Sprout and Scatter:

The unexpected benefit of allowing God's faithful light to shine in your life is that it changes your relationships with others. "But if we walk in the light, as he is in the light, we have fellowship with one another, and the blood of Jesus, his Son, purifies us from all sin" (1 John 1:7). With a clean heart, you love and laugh more. Since the fear of your secrets surfacing is gone, your friendships develop into fellowship. You are free to share the faithful, loving light of God with others.

Think about it:

What attitudes are hidden away in the dark places of your heart?

_____

_____

How can you drag them to the light today?

_____

_____

_____

_____

Prayer Pot:

Lord, I admit I have been unwilling to confront . . .

_____

_____

_____

_____

_____

_____

You cannot put your sins behind you until you face them.

Faithful Doctrine

Today's Seed

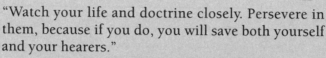

"Watch your life and doctrine closely. Persevere in them, because if you do, you will save both yourself and your hearers."

1 Timothy 4:16

Christianity, Islam, Judaism, Hinduism, and Buddhism. There are many religions. Within each religious group there are factions, orders, sects, schisms, and denominations. Each one has a different view of evolution and creation, and of God and how to approach him. There are varying degrees of morality and ethics, conflicting ideas about sin and good deeds, and incompatible teachings about faith and salvation. We are left with the dilemma: How do we know what to believe? What is the truth?

Orthodox Christianity started with the simple yet profound teachings of Jesus. Then the sermons of Peter and Paul in Acts helped to standardize an accepted body of teachings—or doctrine. Certain fundamental truths are clearly taught in Scripture, such as who Jesus is and his sacrifice for our sins. These doctrines can be held firmly without hesitation.

Dig Deeper:

"Persevere" is translated from the Greek word *epimeno*, meaning *stay with*. It has the idea of taking up residence. Let your doctrine move in with you.

According to George Barna Research there are over 320,000 Protestant churches in America alone. Patrick Johnstone charted the phenomenal growth of evangelical Christians from 29 million in 1960 to over 200 million in 1990. With millions of people from varying backgrounds and cultures, we can't build our beliefs on mere opinion. We need to cling to a faithful doctrine from Scripture.

Peripheral teachings can be argued in love by learned scholars and devoted Christians from different camps. Our job is to understand and be faithful to the essential doctrines and enjoy the debate on lesser ones.

Weed and Water:

Try writing your own statement of faith. (Review Acts 2–3 for ideas.) Then check your actions and feelings against your statement to see if they match. In this second letter to Timothy, Paul encouraged the young pastor not to get so wrapped up in his flock that he failed to evaluate his own life. Timothy was to inspect his actions as well as his thoughts and feelings to make sure they lined up with what he taught. We can do the same. For example, if I say I believe that God is in control, then why am I so worried about _____ ?

Sprout and Scatter:

Knowing the truth helps us reach out to others. When we separate the essentials of doctrine from mere personal preferences or areas of tradition, we are free to express acceptance of those who have differing points of view. We can stick to the main tenets without getting sidetracked in disputes that cause hurt. Some things are worth fighting about, but some things are not. Our acceptance of others encourages them toward the truth in major matters.

Think about it:

Where can you find truth?

_____

List some of the major tenets of the Christian faith.

_____

_____

_____

How does knowing what you believe help you to be faithful?

_____

_____

Prayer Pot:

Father, help me stand firm in the truth even when . . .

_____

_____

_____

_____

_____

_____

Our faith deals with what God says—
not what learned men say.

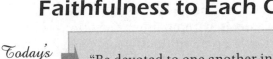

Faithfulness to Each Other

Today's Seed  "Be devoted to one another in brotherly love. Honor one another above yourselves."

Romans 12:10

"I've had it with her! That's it. I give up!"

We've all experienced times when we are so exasperated with another Christian that we feel like stomping up and down—on the person.

Today's seed to be devoted in love and to honor each other follows Paul's discussion of the body of Christ. That's an important context. All Christians form the body of Christ. Each part of the body has a necessary place and purpose. Although some parts of the body may seem important and some may seem worthless, each one deserves honor and respect because of its position in Christ.

As a member of the body, our duty is to be diligent, generous, and cheerful with every other part of the body—regardless of whether or not that body part seems useless or hopeless. In short, our job is to be faithfully devoted. No fellow Christian is without potential because Christ can always work in his or her heart. When we are faithful to each other, we bring out the best in each other and in everyone we meet.

Dig Deeper:

The word translated "honor" means valuable. Our esteem for fellow Christians is to be as great as our honor for our most valuable possession.

Devotion to one another is a result of the new nature that Christ has given us. We can't do it without him. Devotion expresses itself when we don't give up on difficult people and when we recognize that those people are special to God.

Weed and Water:

Imagine a pitcher with a hole in the bottom. The only way you could fill it up would be to hold it under running water. If the amount of water flowing in is greater than the amount going out of the hole, the pitcher will fill and over-flow. For us to overflow in faithfulness to those around us, we must stay under the tap of God's faithfulness. Constant prayer and Bible study will keep us filled. When we stop being filled, we cannot be helpful to others.

Sprout and Scatter:

Think of that Christian who rubs you the wrong way. Only God can fill you with love for that person. Stop now to pray for him or her. You are not able to change that person, but God can change your attitude toward him or her. Determine to faithfully pray for that person this week. Watch out! You may discover your feelings of disgust changing to compassion and brotherly love.

Think about it:

Where do you picture yourself in the body of Christ—as an arm, hand, foot, etc.?

_____

_____

_____

Where do you picture that difficult person fitting in the body of Christ?

_____

_____

_____

Prayer Pot:

Lord, forgive my lack of faithful devotion to . . .

_____

_____

_____

_____

_____

_____

Prayer changes the pray-er.

Gentle Savior

Today's Seed

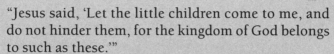

> "Jesus said, 'Let the little children come to me, and do not hinder them, for the kingdom of God belongs to such as these.'"
>
> Matthew 19:14

Nearly every church has a picture of Christ surrounded by a small, yet intimate circle of children. Some are toddlers, some mere babes. But have you ever noticed that the children always look comfortable sitting on his lap or hanging onto his clothes? Perhaps they hadn't yet heard of his position as the Messiah. Or perhaps the eyes of their spiritual understanding had been opened and they recognized Jesus as someone they could trust.

What kind of man was this Jesus who interrupted his day to listen to the giggle or cry of a child? He was not like other adults. The disciples and religious leaders of the day thought children were a nuisance. To Jesus, the children were important. He stopped to kneel on a dust-covered road and demonstrated gentleness towards them. He loved the innocence, faith, and trust that children exude. The Pharisees thought the way to greatness

Dig Deeper:

"Let" is also translated "suffer" or "permit" in other Bible versions. Children have a natural openness to Jesus, and adults have the duty of not getting in their way.

was by strictly following rules. Jesus said that greatness is not found in legalism, but in having a gentle, calm spirit like children.

If Jesus had reacted as the disciples wanted him to, we would not have been given the picture of a gentle savior. Imagine trying to worship or love a person who treated children with contempt! We would fear that person, not love him. In seeing Jesus respond gently to the children we learn that we can come to him too. He is willing to meet us where we are—crushed, excited, or in need of his gentleness!

Background Bulb:

The story of Jesus blessing the children appears in three of the four Gospels: Matthew 19:13–15; Mark 10:13–16; and Luke 18:15–17. It was customary for a Jewish mother to bring her children before a rabbi for blessing. Luke's account reveals parents bringing babies to Jesus just to have him place a hand on them.

Sprout & Scatter:

Children love and need attention, regardless of their behavior. If your church has a children's program or two, consider getting involved in this worthwhile ministry. Doing so will require extra gentleness and energy on your part but remember these words: To share the "good news" with children is to bless them forever.

Think about it:

What are your thoughts about children inheriting the kingdom?

_____

_____

_____

How can you encourage the children in your life to come to the Savior?

_____

_____

_____

Prayer Pot:

Dear Jesus, may I spread your gentleness in this world by . . .

_____

_____

_____

_____

_____

_____

Hold the hand of a child today.

Greatness Can Be Gentle

Today's Seed

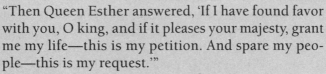

"Then Queen Esther answered, 'If I have found favor with you, O king, and if it pleases your majesty, grant me my life—this is my petition. And spare my people—this is my request.'"

Esther 7:3

Esther's life was in grave danger. As a woman of Jewish heritage, she found herself in a tenuous situation where her people's lives were threatened. King Xerxes, ruler of Persia, had declared that all those of Jewish faith must be annihilated on a single day, including little children.

When God calls a person to greatness, he is not looking for greatness. He is looking for a willing vessel that is ready to be used for his purposes. When she was chosen to become part of the king's harem, Esther probably never guessed that God would use her to save his people.

The king's first wife, Vashti, was banished for disobeying a royal decree. Xerxes was anxious to make an example of his naughty wife, for he feared that wives of other noblemen would despise and disobey their husbands as well.

Enter Esther, one of several young virgins brought in to please

Dig Deeper:
The Hebrew word for "gentleness" denotes fairness and moderation. Esther possessed these qualities and more.

the angry king. Almost immediately, Esther gained favor with the king. She received beauty treatments, special food, and seven maids to attend to her needs. Esther did not reveal her nationality and lived quietly even after she was crowned the new queen.

When events turned grim, Esther began a time of prayer and fasting. After initiating the fast, she demonstrated a gentleness of spirit as she brought her petitions before the king. In speaking so boldly to Xerxes, she risked being killed as a traitor. Yet Esther was more concerned for all the Jews than for her own welfare. In this way, we see that Esther was at a point in her life where pleasing God meant everything. She was a willing vessel.

Background Bulb:

Esther and Ruth are the only two women with entire books in the Bible devoted to them. Both women are revered for their faith, and their gentleness. Both are listed in the lineage of Jesus. God's sovereignty was demonstrated through the story of Esther and her gentle spirit.

Weed and Water:

Have you ever wanted to achieve greatness? To do something great with your life? If you turn your life over to Jesus, there's no telling what he can do through you. Esther was only a young Jewish woman but God used her to save an entire race. Perhaps your family will be saved through the witness you bear.

Think about it:

When making requests or petitions, are you typically gentle or harsh in your tone?

_____

_____

What does God look for in those he uses to serve him?

_____

_____

What would you like to be doing for God?

_____

_____

Prayer Pot:

Dear heavenly Father, forgive me for trying to be great and forgetting to be gentle when . . .

_____

_____

_____

_____

_____

Be ready and willing to let God enable you.

Gentle Surrender

Today's Seed

> "And she [Hannah] made a vow, saying, "O Lord Almighty, if you will only look upon your servant's misery and remember me, and not forget your servant but give her a son, then I will give him to the Lord for all the days of his life, and no razor will ever be used on his head."
>
> 1 Samuel 1:11

Hannah could easily have become a bitter, resentful wife and mother. Although she had prayed many years for a child, she was unable to conceive. To make matters worse, her husband's other wife, Peninnah—who already had several sons and daughters—was constantly trying to provoke Hannah because of her barrenness. Hannah could have felt abandoned by the Lord, but instead she cultivated a spirit of gentleness that resulted in true surrender to God and self-control with others.

God honored her by blessing her with a son, whom she named Samuel. When Samuel was weaned, Hannah kept her word and brought Samuel to the temple to be raised by Eli, the high priest.

A gentle person is one who has placed herself under God's control and is never out of control with others. Hannah is a perfect

Dig Deeper:

"Give" in today's seed means to bestow, grant, permit, lend, or entrust. Giving by its very nature implies surrendering that which belongs to us.

example. First, she chose not to retaliate against Peninnah, trusting that the Lord would right the wrong committed against her. Second, when Eli spied Hannah on her knees in the temple, mouthing words with no sound, he assumed she was drunk. Rather than responding in anger with a sharp rebuke, Hannah gently explained that she was pouring out her heart to God in prayer because she was deeply troubled at her barrenness.

Several years later when Hannah brought Samuel to the temple and presented him to the Lord, she did not cry as most mothers would have. Instead, she sang a song of praise to God! God blessed Hannah for her gentle spirit by giving her three more sons and two daughters.

Weed and Water:

Surrender says "yes" to God and "no" to self. Look closely at those areas you have not given fully to God. Remember that true surrender causes us to take our hands off the person or situation and place that person or thing into God's capable hands. Hannah knew Samuel was a gift on loan from God, and she trusted God to take care of him. What do you have trouble trusting God about? Imagine placing that person or thing into God's huge and capable hands.

Sprout and Scatter:

Suppose Hannah had reneged on her commitment to present Samuel to the Lord, thinking that she couldn't bear to give him up. Israel would have been deprived of a wonderful spiritual leader. Imagine if Hannah had become angry and resentful after giving Samuel to the Lord. Her life would have been poisoned with bitterness that would have spilled over to her family and friends. When we surrender our lives into God's control, blessings flow out of our gentle spirits into those around us.

Think about it:

How was Hannah gentle?

_____

_____

_____

How will you implement a gentle spirit of surrender in your family?

_____

_____

_____

_____

Prayer Pot:

Lord, cause me to be gentle and to surrender . . .

_____

_____

_____

_____

_____

_____

When we surrender everything to God, we gain more than we give.

A Gentle Witness!

Today's Seed

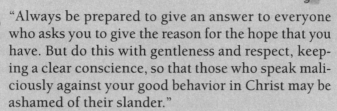

"Always be prepared to give an answer to everyone who asks you to give the reason for the hope that you have. But do this with gentleness and respect, keeping a clear conscience, so that those who speak maliciously against your good behavior in Christ may be ashamed of their slander."

1 Peter 3:15b–16

Think back to conversations you had with Christians prior to your conversion. Were you clobbered over the head with Bible verses, told to repent, or called a big sinner? Hopefully, the person or persons who led you to Christ had more tact than this, but if not, you have the chance to do things differently as you sprinkle spiritual salt.

While John the Baptist got away with shouting, "You brood of vipers!" to the Pharisees, it's unlikely that his methods would work well in our neighborhoods. When we talk about our faith, we should do so gently by being respectful of our listeners.

Always being ready to give an answer implies that those around us are asking questions. In Peter's day believers could be questioned

Dig Deeper:

The phrase "to give an answer" is *apologia* in Greek. Our answer or testimony to the world is a verbal defense, or a reasoned statement or argument.

casually by friends and neighbors or formally by government authorities opposed to Christians. Today we run into people at our jobs, in school, or even at the store who watch us and wonder about the difference they see in our words and actions.

Christians have an underlying attitude of hope that non-Christians find puzzling. People will want to know more about it. Today's seed tells us to speak with gentleness so that no one will have a reason to doubt our answers to their questions. So respond gently and respectfully, pointing out that it's Christ alone that makes us different!

Weed and Water:

Most of us feel more comfortable being silent about our Christianity. We want to live in such as way that non-Christians are drawn to Christ so that we have a silent witness, but we end up appearing like we think we're perfect. The result is that non-Christians see us as phonies or hypocrites. Are you guilty of this? Ask for God's forgiveness and courage to be real and vulnerable, sharing your struggles.

Sprout and Scatter:

Did God save you from a life of alcoholism or help you overcome feelings of self-contempt? If so, your past is worth sharing because it reveals your humanity, your need for grace. God saves us all from eternal damnation but he also saves us from ourselves. Next time you want to tell someone what to do or not do, begin your words with a reference to your own sins. Let the Holy Spirit salt your speech with gentleness and give you his words so that your witnessing will be done in good taste.

Think about it:

How does your testimony hold up to the challenge given in today's seed?

_____

In what ways can you be more gentle in sharing your faith?

_____

_____

When was the last time you shared your faith or prayed with an unbeliever?

_____

_____

Prayer Pot:

Dear Lord, let my words be well seasoned, well timed, and gentle as I . . .

_____

_____

_____

_____

_____

Gentle witnesses leave the world thirsty for more.

He Shall Gently Lead

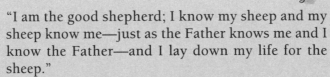

Today's Seed

"I am the good shepherd; I know my sheep and my sheep know me—just as the Father knows me and I know the Father—and I lay down my life for the sheep."

John 10:14–15

Everyone loves the image of Jesus as a good shepherd. It's a comforting picture.

In John 10, Jesus states his deity when he describes the relationship he has with the Father. He also shares how much he cares for those who follow him. He (meaning Jesus) says he will lay down his life for the sheep (meaning us). Jesus' sacrifice has given us access to the Father. It is nearly impossible to grasp the kind of love Jesus has for us, but we must believe that it is so.

To grow spiritually, Christians need tender care and vigilant supervision just as if they were sheep. God has ordained pastors or godly leaders to care for the flock through sermons, encouragement, prayer, and correction.

The shepherd's tasks, however, are not the same as the hired hand's tasks. A hired hand is in it for the money. He will feed the

Dig Deeper:

"Shepherd," as used by Jesus is the Greek word *poimen*. We typically think of pastors as figurative shepherds with the responsibility of urging the people toward obedience to God.

sheep but leave when his shift is over. Our Gentle Shepherd is ever-present and never takes a day off.

Like sheep we bear our Shepherd's mark and belong to him. He takes a personal interest in our health and growth. Consequently, Jesus demonstrates his mercy and grace when one of us strays into danger. The Shepherd's rod and staff are never used to beat us into submission but to lead us in obedience. With Jesus as our Shepherd we experience benevolent care and guidance.

Background Bulb:

Sheep are known for their stupidity. Even if food and water are nearby, sheep have trouble finding it. Sheep need a shepherd, someone who will lead them to the food, protect them from the elements, and keep them safe from predators. Sheep have a tendency to stray, to be fearful, timid, and stubborn. They require constant supervision and care. The character and diligence of the shepherd has a direct influence on the health of the flock.

Sprout and Scatter:

Are you a shepherd over anyone? You are if you are a mother. Shepherding means leading a person toward spiritual growth in Christ using Scripture as a tool to encourage, not a weapon to punish. If you have no biological children, you can shepherd by mentoring younger women. We can share examples of God's leading in our lives and the consequences of not listening to the shepherd. Whomever God has called you to lead or teach, do so gently.

Think about it:

Why do Christians need a shepherd?

_____

_____

_____

How has Jesus acted as Gentle Shepherd in your life?

_____

_____

_____

How can you gently lead others to a deeper faith in
Christ?

_____

_____

Prayer Pot:

Dear Lord, help me to shepherd . . .

_____

_____

_____

_____

_____

His rod and his staff, they gently
comfort me.

A Gentle Answer

Today's Seed

> "A gentle answer turns away wrath, but a harsh word stirs up anger."
>
> Proverbs 15:1

In 1915 John D. Rockefeller addressed a group of angry strikers at the Colorado Fuel and Iron Company. The air was filled with hatred for the wealthy man who controlled the company. Instead of inciting violence, Rockefeller addressed the men as friends, saying, "This is a red-letter day in my life. It is the first time I have ever had the good fortune to meet the representatives of the employees of this great company, its officers and superintendents, together, and I can assure you that I am proud to be here."

Obviously, Rockefeller had learned the fine art of making friends out of enemies. Suppose that he began his speech in defense mode, justifying himself, attacking, or hurling insults. Anger would have erupted into violence and he may not have escaped with his life.

When you face people who are angry with you, do you remain cool, calm, and collected? Or do you react harshly? Today's seed gives wisdom for our interactions with angry people.

Dig Deeper:

Heat, rage, anger, poison, and hot displeasure all indicate a person's wrath. "Wrath" comes from the Hebrew word *chemah*. Anger between people is poison to relationships.

A soft answer contains the argument, often stopping further attack. When you refuse to engage in verbal combat, you usually disarm your attacker. God calls his children to "be quick to listen, slow to speak and slow to become angry, for man's anger does not bring about the righteous life that God desires" (James 1:19–20).

Background Bulb:

Satan, the ultimate deceiver, began the war of words in the Garden of Eden when he lied to Eve about God's rules. Satan twisted God's words and poisoned humankind's relationship with God and with each other. The first recorded argument between a husband and wife occurred when Adam blamed Eve and Eve blamed the serpent. Don't let yourself fall prey to the evil one. He wants us to argue and fight.

Weed and Water:

Have you ever tried to argue in a whisper? You can't do it. It's equally hard to argue with someone who insists on answering gently. Raising your voice and using harsh words almost always triggers an angry response. To turn away wrath and seek peace, choose gentle words and speak in a quiet voice with a calm tone.

Think about it:

Describe the last time you were in an argument.

_____

_____

How might that confrontation have been different if those involved had answered gently?

_____

List ways you could respond calmly in a volatile situation.

🐞 _____

🐞 _____

🐞 _____

Prayer Pot:
Lord, let my words bring peace and gentleness to . . .

_____

_____

_____

_____

_____

_____

To answer an angry person with a harsh word is to blow on an already smoldering fire.

Horizontal Gentleness

Today's Seed

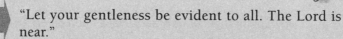

"Let your gentleness be evident to all. The Lord is near."

Philippians 4:5

The telephone rings. A friend wants to chat but your children (or grandchildren) begin fighting as soon as you say "Hello." In five seconds your countenance and attitude plummet from "Praise the Lord!" to "Knock it off!"

We wouldn't dream of letting others see or hear the real us, so we cover the receiver as we yell at the noisemakers. We smile to our friend while we scowl at our children. Our families see the real us, and gentleness is not always evident to them. Often we excuse our harsh behavior as unimportant, giving more effort to relationships with our friends, with people who are like us, with acquaintances we want to impress, or with God.

Paul, the writer of today's seed, says, "Not so fast! Be gentle to everyone! Behave as though Christ were beside you." Too often we think our vertical relationship with the Father is good, but we don't notice our horizontal relationships are full of muck. Our gentleness must be evident to everyone or it's worthless. It's hypocrisy.

Dig Deeper:

The verb translated "be known [evident]" is in the passive voice. This indicates that we should not put on a show of gentleness, but by being ourselves others should see gentleness. It should be part of the fabric of our lives.

Background Bulb:

In the verses preceding today's seed, Paul names two women and pleads with them to be unified. Apparently, they were embroiled in a dispute that was not a matter of right or wrong but of differing opinions. In short, their personalities clashed. Paul urged them to give up the petty fight and to show consideration and gentleness to each other on the basis of their love for Christ. Paul wanted them to be gentle with each other so the focus of those around them would be drawn upward to the cross.

Weed and Water:

Imagine that Christ is seated next to you at all times, not just on Sunday mornings. When you encounter those you dislike, Jesus can spot your bouts of harshness. No doubt you'd cringe in his presence and strive to be more gentle. Ask the Holy Spirit to give you his power today to react in gentle, Christlike ways. Horizontal gentleness won't happen without the Holy Spirit's power and effort.

Think about it:

Why are we tempted to be more gentle with outsiders than with family members?

_____

_____

What can you do when you find your gentleness waning?

_____

_____

Why do we need to be concerned about horizontal gentleness?

_____

Prayer Pot:

Lord, forgive me for my lack of gentleness with . . .

_____

_____

_____

_____

_____

The cross intersects the horizontal and vertical.

Gentleness Is Love in Action

Today's Seed

"As apostles of Christ we could have been a burden to you, but we were gentle among you, like a mother caring for her little children."

1 Thessalonians 2:6b–7

Many powerful people get what they want. They take great pride in wielding their assertiveness even if underlings are trampled on in the process. Those on their way to the top often use the phrase "the end justifies the means."

Paul and his fellow apostles were on their way to the top too. They were heaven bound and full of authority. They had the power of the Holy Spirit backing their ministry, though, not a huge bankroll in their pockets. While witnessing in the city of Thessalonica, Paul instructed his men not to become a burden to the Christians living there. He did not ask or expect the Christians to feed and clothe him while he worked among them. It is believed that Paul even kept his day job as a tent maker to avoid the appearance of being greedy. He did this because he wanted the focus to remain on caring for the new believers.

To carry out their ministry in a sincere, effective manner, Paul,

Dig Deeper:
"To nurse" as a mother is to nourish or nurture along; to feed. The root form for this Greek word is trepho, a verb, and verbs are words of action.

Timothy, and Silas nurtured the people of Thessalonica. Quite possibly, the disciples may have hosted dinners for the people or helped them with their work. In verses 8 and 9 Paul continues: "We loved you so much that we were delighted to share with you not only the gospel of God but our lives as well, because you had become so dear to us. Surely, you remember, brothers, our toil and hardship." The disciples possessed more Bible knowledge than others in the town but they remained servants, living gently in all situations.

Weed and Water:

We don't usually think of men in the role of mother or nurse, but even Jesus assumed a nurturing role. Pastors and lay leaders (men and women alike) must be servants who nourish others spiritually. Check to see that you are not a burden in your ministry, taking from others more than you are giving.

Sprout and Scatter:

In the Christian life, it is more important to encourage spiritual growth in others than to establish a personal fiefdom. Ask God to send those who have ministry needs to you. Don't overlook the needs of little ones who are tugging at your side. Offer to lend support and mentor those who are new in the faith. You might even want to become a prayer warrior for a new ministry in your church.

Think about it:

How might you be a burden to someone?

_____

_____

How does using others affect our testimony as believers?

_____

_____

How can you avoid becoming "power hungry" in ministry?

_____

_____

Prayer Pot:

Father, forgive me if I have misused my power over . . .

_____

_____

_____

_____

_____

_____

Be a blessing, not a burden.

Gentleness and Meekness

Today's Seed

> "Blessed are the meek: for they shall inherit the earth."
>
> Matthew 5:5

Do you consider yourself to be a meek person?

Many times we avoid the word "meekness" because we think it implies wimpiness. But meekness is a good quality and a part of gentleness.

Christ is the ultimate example of meekness. He bore our sins, our punishment, and death on the cross without picking up a weapon to defend himself or seeking revenge. He wasn't weak. He willingly gave his life that we might enter into a relationship with his Father. (See Isaiah 53.) Jesus could have gotten off the cross and called the angels to whisk him away, yet he chose to fulfill the will of God for our sake. Jesus didn't die because he was too weak to save himself. He died because he was too great not to save us.

Weakness (as defined by Webster's Dictionary) is character that lacks strength, firmness, or vigor. Jesus dispels the myth that a gentle disposition is for wimps because he possessed all the power in the world yet chose not to use it. Weakness also implies

Dig Deeper:

"Blessed," as used in the Beatitudes, comes from a word that means fortunate, well-off, or happy.

a defective quality in a person's character. Christ will never be found lacking; he was perfect.

The Bible promises that the meek shall inherit the earth. Walking in meekness requires two attributes: (1) a willingness to rely on God as the source of one's strength and (2) a moldable heart. Meek and gentle Christians are not harsh, aggressive, or domineering. They are strong enough to admit their need for Christ.

Weed and Water:

Meekness, not weakness, is the mark of a true Christian. Athletes who pray before the beginning of a football game and also those who bow their heads in thanks for victory realize that their talents and strengths are God-given. Being on our knees before God demonstrates our lowly status before a holy God and makes us meek.

Sprout and Scatter:

First Samuel 16:7 says, "But the Lord said to Samuel, 'do not consider his appearance or his height, for I have rejected him. The Lord does not look at the things man looks at. Man looks at the outward appearance, but the Lord looks at the heart.'" Befriend the timid, overlooked people in your church or office. Stoop down to address a child who sits or plays alone day after day.

Think about it:

What made Jesus endure death in our place?

_____

_____

_____

What attitudes are involved in being meek?

_____

_____

Why should we desire meekness?

_____

_____

Prayer Pot:

Lord, thank you for caring about the meek, especially . . .

_____

_____

_____

_____

_____

_____

A meek person is stronger than she looks.

Gentle Communication

Today's Seed

> "To slander no one, to be peaceable and considerate, and to show true humility toward all men."
> Titus 3:2

In the world of professional wrestling, fighters and promoters earn millions by trash talking, brawling, and taking their opponents down. Occasionally fans become so frenzied that they end up getting in on the action. When this happens, chairs fly through the air and otherwise sensible spectators climb into the ring. And today's talk shows are seldom any better than wrestling. Slanderous and insulting words incite violence.

Although Jesus raised his voice a time or two during his ministry, he remained in control as he responded to those who sought to trap him. The Pharisees enjoyed baiting Jesus and twisting his words. Jesus called them a brood of vipers! (Matthew 23:33). He spoke harshly to the sin he saw (their hypocrisy) but did not put others down or try to make himself look better. He did not engage in arguments for the sake of arguing as some do.

Today's seed in the King James translation reads: "To speak evil of no man, to be no brawlers, but gentle, showing all meekness

Dig Deeper:

The Hebrew word *dibbah* means defaming, evil report, infamy, and slander. We are not to speak evil of others no matter how tempting it is.

unto all men." Followers of Christ ought to illustrate gentleness through their words and actions not just to other Christians but to everyone. To do so we must use our words to edify and not tear down. We must use self-control in our speech.

Weed and Water:

In real life we are no different than those trash-talking wrestlers when we tear down our family members or neighbors with gossip, half-truths, or lies. Sometimes we start arguments over the stupidest things, or we fail to listen long enough to hear the other person's side in a conflict. Today, time yourself and see how many minutes you can go without saying something that might be unwholesome. Be silent if you don't have anything good to say.

Sprout and Scatter:

Focus on building others up with your words. When you hear someone being put down, get involved. Don't look the other way. Say something positive about the person who is being discussed. Walk away from the water cooler if everyone is blasting the supervisor today. Make it a habit to say one nice thing about your spouse each day.

Think about it:

How have you caused dissension in your family or church?

_____

_____

Who can you build up with your words?

_____

_____

What will you say or do differently in the coming weeks?

_____

_____

Prayer Pot:

Jesus, make my words gentle when . . .

_____

_____

_____

_____

_____

_____

"A perverse woman stirs up dissension, and a gossip separates friends."
—Proverbs 16:28

Resolve

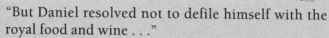

Today's Seed

> "But Daniel resolved not to defile himself with the royal food and wine . . ."
>
> Daniel 1:8

Have you ever noticed how determined we are to do well when we start something new? We register for school and trot off to the bookstore to purchase not only the texts but also spiral notebooks, three-ring binders, and comfort-grip pens. We decide to sew a new outfit and have a grand time choosing fabric and matching trim. Or we change our hairdo and buy all the necessary products to keep it up. Oh, beginnings are wonderful. When embarking upon projects we enjoy, we start with a bang.

What about when we're faced with tasks we're not excited about?

Enter resolve. Resolve is the first step on the path to self-control. Resolve is a conscious decision. It takes resolve to start and *continue* tasks that look rough. It takes resolve and the help of the Holy Spirit to make decisions concerning right and wrong.

Daniel found himself facing such a decision. He could do the easy thing and eat the food put before him, although it was not

Dig Deeper:

The Hebrew word for resolve means to put, place, determine, or name. Naming something determines its meaning based on its characteristics. Our resolve determines our character.

kosher and had been offered to idols. Or he could stand up for his beliefs. He resolved not to defile himself, to stick to what he knew was right regardless of the consequences.

Once we understand Scripture's teachings, it's up to us to make the deliberate choice to obey. Resolve starts with an inner determination to obey God. Daniel loved God enough not to want to displease him. He faced an issue of obedience and faith and was willing to suffer for his righteous decision.

Background Bulb:

Daniel was one of the brightest young men chosen from Israel to be groomed by their captors for the Babylonian king's service. The idea was to fill these young men with Babylonian culture and use them to keep their countrymen under control. Daniel's determination not to defile himself with the food forbidden by the law of Moses was only the beginning of Daniel's lifetime resolve to serve God.

Weed and Water:

When we believe God wants us to cut back on this or stop that, we must be mindful not to allow our restraint to look and sound like condemnation of others who are not so led. Be quietly obedient. Gently voice your resolve while saying that God has led you to do this.

Think about it:

What was Daniel's reaction when faced with the decision to choose between right and wrong?

_____

_____

What circumstances cause you to break your resolve?

_____

_____

What circumstances push you to dig your heels in and stick to your resolve?

_____

_____

Prayer Pot:

Lord, help me resolve to . . .

_____

_____

_____

_____

_____

"The man who is tenacious of purpose in a rightful cause is not shaken from his firm resolve by the frenzy of his fellow citizens clamoring for what is wrong, or by the tyrant's threatening countenance."

—Horace, from _Epodes_, iii, l. r.

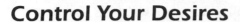

Control Your Desires

Today's Seed

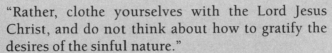

"Rather, clothe yourselves with the Lord Jesus Christ, and do not think about how to gratify the desires of the sinful nature."

Romans 13:14

It's amazing how some women who never really had the self-control to take good care of their bodies gain firm control when they become expectant mothers. Suddenly vegetables look good and milk tastes great. They exercise, drink plenty of water, take their vitamins, and get enough rest.

What causes the change? The knowledge of that precious life within their wombs.

Similarly, believers have Christ's life within them from the moment they accept his offer of salvation. From there they must work at making Christian values a habitual part of life. Godliness doesn't automatically follow conversion just as a healthy lifestyle doesn't automatically follow knowledge of a pregnancy.

Healthy spiritual living involves daily decisions to wear the clothes of righteousness that Christ gives us. We do that by recognizing that he is king over every part of us. Unfortunately, our bodies don't understand that our spirits are subject to Christ, so

Dig Deeper:

The word "gratify" is added by the translators to the NIV version for clarity. The Greek text says, "Do not think about" your human nature with its frailties physically or morally, and passions ("desires of the sinful nature").

our flesh craves that which our spirit opposes. (See Galatians 5:17.)

Clothing ourselves in the Lord Jesus Christ means we learn what he wants for us. We choose to obey him so often his ways become our habits. The more he controls us, the less we're controlled by our sinful physical and emotional desires. Imagine yourself throwing off bad habits as you would old clothing and dressing in new, glamorous clothes of righteousness.

Weed and Water:

What do you crave? Control? Praise from others? Gossip? Sweets? Romantic fantasies? Take notice of what your mind, emotions, and body crave that is not pleasing to God. If you aren't sure whether a craving is right or wrong, check your Bible to see what God says about it. Once you identify God's view, submit that craving to his control. Discipline your mind not to think about it.

Sprout and Scatter:

Help a friend, your husband, or your children overcome a destructive habit that gratifies the sinful nature by challenging them to a habit-breaking contest. Tell each other about the habit you each want to break. Then devise checks, balances, and a rewards system for changing that behavior. Be sure to substitute the destructive habit with something that will honor God.

Think about it:

With what are Christians to clothe themselves?

_____

_____

_____

_____

List some thoughts you should put out of your mind.

_____

_____

_____

Prayer Pot:

Lord, help me to take control of my flesh by . . .

_____

_____

_____

_____

_____

_____

God plus you equals a majority, even against the many desires of the flesh.

It's My Own Fault

Today's Seed

"But each one is tempted when, by his own evil desire, he is dragged away and enticed."

James 1:14

Years ago, comedian Flip Wilson made famous the phrase "The devil made me do it." Although Satan can be blamed for his share of troublemaking, we are adept at getting ourselves into messes. We gravitate toward evil, and no one ever has to teach us to do wrong things or lie to cover them up.

Although we eventually realize there are consequences to our actions, that doesn't stop us. We simply weigh our actions more carefully, deciding if the commission of the act is worth the risk of getting caught. If we are caught, we shift the blame. We even have the nerve to blame God for some of our misfortune.

The self-control issue of today's seed has to do with the necessity for us to control our own evil desires that drag us away from God's pure ones for us. God does not tempt us. We allow ourselves to be enticed by listening to voices other than his—voices that scream at us about what our flesh wants:

Dig Deeper:
The word "entice" comes from a Greek word meaning to entrap, allure, and beguile.

"Have one more piece of pie; you'll exercise tomorrow."

"Flirt with that handsome married neighbor; flirting is harmless."

"Give full vent to your anger; that no-good person should suffer too."

Imagine temptation to sin as the devil along the highway trying to flag you down. First, he tries to get your attention. Second, he persuades you to stop. Third, he lures you out of your car with attractive bait. Finally, he grabs you and drags you away into sin. Notice you took the first three steps of your own free will.

Weed and Water:

What looks tempting? Are you continuing to look at that person or thing with longing? If so, you can easily be led away by your desires. Pinpoint the sinful desires in your life and pray daily that God will replace them with his desires for you. Look up Scripture promises that relate to your issues, write them on note cards, and meditate upon them.

Sprout and Scatter:

Many people succumb to their bad habits and are then condemned by other Christians. It is possible to love the person and hate the sin. Don't be judgmental, especially if you never struggled with a friend's particular sin. If you have dealt with her issue, share honestly about it. Be a listening ear, visit her when she's discouraged, and be ready to give a loving, biblical answer when the conversation warrants it.

Think about it:

List two areas where you need more self-control.

_____

_____

What kind of a "road sign" can you use to remind you not to stop your spiritual car?

_____

_____

_____

_____

_____

Prayer Pot:

Lord, please help me tackle and gain control of . . .

_____

_____

_____

_____

_____

_____

If God tells us to control certain areas of our lives, that means we can.

I Want That

Today's Seed

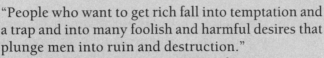

"People who want to get rich fall into temptation and a trap and into many foolish and harmful desires that plunge men into ruin and destruction."

1 Timothy 6:9

Living in a society of wealth and abundance, we often find ourselves desiring the "best," especially when we seem to be the only ones going without. *Everyone has a cell phone except me*, we grumble miserably. *Why is everyone driving a newer car than mine? Why does everyone live in a bigger house, wear better clothes, and sport more beautiful jewelry than I do?*

The desire to be rich and have nice things is a hard one to knock. We can't ignore money because we need it to survive. But we also can't listen to society, which says, "Charge it! Borrow it! Lease it! Refinance it!" We have to find a balance.

For example, working overtime will show a gain on a paycheck, but too much time away from family can strain a marriage and make parents lose touch with their kids. Living in a bigger house will give a family room to spread out and entertain guests, but it also means higher utility bills and the need for more furniture and

Dig Deeper:

"Trap" means being snared or fastened by a noose. Faulty business deals and bad investments leave us hanging precariously to our own ruin.

upkeep. A newer, more expensive car may be dependable and impressive to friends, but it could also come with lower gas mileage and a higher insurance bill, not to mention that new car loan.

Before going for bigger and better, evaluate your reasons for the change. God promised to meet your *need*, not your *greed*. Submit your desire to be rich to God and follow his plans for gaining wealth.

Background Bulb:

Abraham was rich. Solomon was rich. Job was rich. God allowed key figures in the Bible to have wealth; there's nothing wrong with money itself. However the desire for riches must not control us. The gathering of wealth must not be our focus. The rich young ruler went away from Christ sorrowful because he loved money more than he loved God. Jesus taught that it's hard for a rich man to enter heaven for this very same reason. (See Matthew 19:16–24.)

Weed and Water:

Refuse to spend money on that which you can live without. Make a list with two columns, one labeled "Needs" and the other labeled "Wants." Honestly assess your lifestyle and write down everything on which you spend money, listing each thing under the proper category. For at least one month spend money only on your needs and save the money you would have spent on your wants.

Think about it:

How much time each day do you spend acquiring wealth?

_____

_____

How does your answer compare to time spent on other daily events?

_____

_____

What can you do to better balance the time?

_____

_____

Prayer Pot:

Lord, forgive my focus on . . .

_____

_____

_____

_____

_____

_____

We spend money we don't have on things we don't need to impress people we don't like.

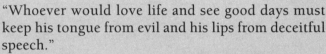

Watch Your Mouth

Today's Seed

"Whoever would love life and see good days must keep his tongue from evil and his lips from deceitful speech."

1 Peter 3:10

It has been proven scientifically that men and women differ greatly in the amount of conversation they participate in.

As preschool girls we engage in conversation using many more words than our male counterparts, who are using their vocal cords to make car and airplane noises. As we reach our teen years, girls spend hours on the phone while the boys engage in the grunts of sports competition or short exclamations over video games.

The adult years don't change much. Women use thousands of words per day, whereas men use only hundreds. It's easy to see how we women could fall into the trap of speaking the wrong things! We feel the need to talk and be heard, but we often end up gossiping or complaining instead of just keeping our mouths shut.

Dig Deeper:

Deceitful speech is meant to trick the hearer. When the speaker allows the listener to come away from what has been said with the wrong idea, the speaker has spoken deceitfully.

Today's seed reminds us that the control of our tongue is directly related to our happiness and contentment with life. We don't need to respond to all the little things family members say or do that bother us. We don't need to talk about other people in a negative way. Controlling what comes out of our mouths will contribute to our enjoyment of life.

Who doesn't want to love life and look forward to good days here on earth?

Background Bulb:

It's interesting that James writes strong statements about the control of the tongue (James 1:26; 3:5–9). James was Jesus' half brother. Imagine growing up in the same household with Jesus! James watched Jesus up close, and what James later wrote, he had learned firsthand. James's words about the control of the tongue were borne of his closeness with the Savior, who always knew what to say and when to say it.

Sprout and Scatter:

Challenge children and teenagers to avoid deceit by being specific when you ask questions. Instead of asking, "Did you do your homework?" rephrase the question as, "Did you do all of your homework?" A child who would answer "yes" to the first question (because he finished his grammar but not his math), would have to answer "no" to the second question. You may also ask the child or teen, "What do you think I'm asking you?" His answer to this question should clarify what he truly heard you say.

Think about it:

When was the last time you intentionally allowed someone to misunderstand you?

_____

_____

Why did you do this?

_____

_____

How can you avoid the fear of negative consequences and speak without deceit?

_____

_____

Prayer Pot:

Lord, forgive me for deceitful words and stop me when my tongue . . .

_____

_____

_____

_____

_____

"Set a guard over my mouth, O Lord;
keep watch over the door of my lips."
—Psalm 141:3

Run!

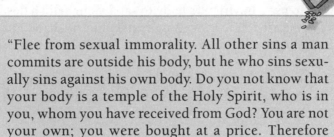

Today's Seed

"Flee from sexual immorality. All other sins a man commits are outside his body, but he who sins sexually sins against his own body. Do you not know that your body is a temple of the Holy Spirit, who is in you, whom you have received from God? You are not your own; you were bought at a price. Therefore honor God with your body."

1 Corinthians 6:18–20

Before marriage, one of the hardest struggles dating couples face is that of remaining sexually pure. They often think, *once we're married, sexual sin won't be a problem anymore.* That's a lie. It's true that married couples no longer have to worry about premarital sex; instead they face new struggles and temptations. For example, a husband is drawn to an attractive coworker, or a wife rejects her mate in the bedroom, opting for sleep rather than intimacy.

Human nature is ornery and contrary. Whatever is right to do, our flesh pulls us in the opposite direction. We probably wouldn't even obey the command to replenish the earth had God not put so much pleasure in the sex act!

Dig Deeper:
"Flee" literally means to run away from, as if escaping from danger.

Selfishness plays a large part in sexual sin. When we're single, it tempts us to use a boyfriend's body to satisfy our selfish desires. When we're married, it tempts us to neglect our husband's physical and emotional needs, or to focus our attentions on another man.

Married or single, our bodies do not belong to us. They belong to God. To misuse them is to tarnish something our Creator made and loves.

Weed and Water:

Before you act on a desire, ask yourself: *Is this harmful? Will it enslave me, hurt someone, or detract from my Christian witness?* If your answer is "yes," run! If single, change the radio station away from suggestive or sexual love songs. Limit the time you spend alone with your date. If married, make every effort not to be alone with a man other than your husband, regardless of how harmless you may think it is. If your husband wants some attention in the bedroom and you are not in the mood, rethink your refusal. Are you being selfish?

Sprout and Scatter:

Single and married women can help each other control the area of sexual immorality. Single women can help their married friends by babysitting their children for a weekend, giving the couple extended time alone to celebrate their marriage and meet each other's emotional and sexual needs. The married friend can, in turn, encourage her single friend to remain abstinent until marriage by supporting the activities she's in and befriending her when she's lonely.

Think about it:

What activities are you involved in that could lead to sexual immorality?

_____
_____
_____

How can you honor God with your body?

_____
_____
_____
_____

Prayer Pot:

Lord, help me honor you with my body as I . . .

_____
_____
_____
_____
_____
_____

"I know only that what is moral is what you feel good after and what is immoral is what you feel bad after."
—Ernest Hemingway,
Death in the Afternoon

Self-Control with Food

Today's Seed

"If you find honey, eat just enough—too much of it, and you will vomit."

Proverbs 25:16

We hear it all the time.

"Watch what you eat."

"Cut down on fat and salt."

"Be sure you're eating your fruits and vegetables."

"Avoid caffeine."

From books and articles to television commercials, specials, and news segments, we are bombarded with cautionary information about our diet.

For some reason, many of us don't heed the advice. Maybe it's overkill—we hear so many admonishments that we tune them out. Sometimes the advice is conflicting. Perhaps our pride leads us to believe that since we haven't yet felt the effects of poor diet, we never will. It's true, however, that our bodies are the temple of God and what we do to them and put into them is important.

Dig Deeper:

"Just enough" comes from the word "sufficient," which is the same word used in Deuteronomy 15:8 when God tells his people to lend the poor whatever will meet their needs.

Today's seed makes the whole issue of self-control over our diets seem so easy. Just don't eat too much. No problem, right?

Wrong! When it comes to food, our appetites often tell us we can't have too much of a good thing. It's hard not to overeat—harder for some than for others, perhaps, but hard nonetheless. But in the end it all comes down to balance and moderation. In other words, we have to exercise self-control. We have to learn to eat an appropriate portion, then walk away. Self-control is the only cure for the disease of the overactive fork.

Background Bulb:

When God rained down a heavenly food for the children of Israel in Exodus 16:12–25, they were to gather only as much manna as they could use in one day. Manna that was saved always spoiled. Before the Sabbath the people were to gather two days' worth. Only on the Sabbath would the manna gathered the day before stay fresh. In this way control of the appetite was linked to total dependence upon and obedience to God.

Weed and Water:

For one week, make it a project to add a question to your prayer over your meals and snacks. Ask God, "Should I eat this? If so, how much of it should I eat?" Be sensitive to what you feel God's answer is. Eat slowly, listen to your body, and stop when you feel full. Then choose one area and start paying attention and controlling that thing—drinking enough water, cutting down on salt, limiting sweets—in monthly efforts to control your appetite.

Think about it:

What areas of your appetite do you need to control?

_____

_____

_____

Why do you think these areas are out of control?

_____

_____

What do you plan to do about this?

_____

_____

Prayer Pot:

Lord, please help me control my appetite in the area(s) of . . .

_____

_____

_____

_____

_____

_____

"One must eat to live, and not live to eat."

—Molièrè, from *Amphitryon*, Act III, i, 1666

The Broken Wall

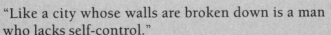

Today's Seed

"Like a city whose walls are broken down is a man who lacks self-control."

Proverbs 25:28

"Boss, I was only ten minutes late."

"But, honey, it was on sale."

"I only missed the payment date by two days."

A little white lie, a stretching of the truth, a slight oversight, a good excuse. However you look at it, the outcome is the same. The problem that results from each of the above statements if left unchecked is a "broken down wall," a breach that can allow a host of other ills to enter. The old adage is true—one thing does lead to another.

We open ourselves to additional problems in our lives when we allow any area to be out of control. We procrastinate and wonder why opportunity never seems to knock. We overspend and can't figure out why the ends don't meet. We tell lies and wonder why no one trusts us. We're irresponsible and wonder why no one ever gives us a break. In each case, one bad decision leads to another.

Dig Deeper:

The Hebrew word for self-control in this seed appears only once in the Old Testament. It means to enclose or rule over one's own spirit.

Once those additional things add up, we look back in shock, often not realizing we tore the wall down ourselves and allowed those problems in.

Self-control builds protective walls. By not procrastinating, we eventually will get things accomplished. Paying bills rather than making them will lead to financial freedom. Telling the truth will result in good relationships. Exercise self-control. Build up your walls.

Weed and Water:

We cannot stop negative things from happening to us. We can, however, do our best not to bring negative things upon ourselves. When our appetites tempt us to get out of control, we build protective walls by deciding not to satisfy those appetites. We gain mastery over our passions only by subjecting them to the will of Christ.

Sprout and Scatter:

Help your friends build walls. Come together and decide to be accountable to one another to control your passions and appetites. Do not suggest a calorie-ridden dessert to the friend who is overweight. Help the procrastinator by breaking the tasks into tiny bits, each with a recognizable, attainable goal. Make a financial plan for the spender. At the end of three months, come together and have a praise party about all God's done to build your walls.

Think about it:

What negative circumstances in your life are the results of cracks in your self-control wall?

_____

_____

_____

How can you control the character flaw that allowed that breach to occur?

_____

_____

_____

Prayer Pot:

Lord, help me build my walls in the area of . . .

_____

_____

_____

_____

_____

_____

Good self-control walls make good neighbors.

Get It Together

Today's Seed

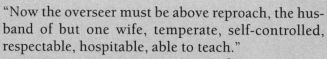

"Now the overseer must be above reproach, the husband of but one wife, temperate, self-controlled, respectable, hospitable, able to teach."

1 Timothy 3:2

Suppose your boss flirted with every man she met, never put anything away and then blamed others when she couldn't find it, yelled at her husband because she had a bad day, never invited anyone into her home, and didn't teach her kids to do anything for themselves.

She would not be a good leader. No one would look up to her. Her family would not find her very lovable. If we were in her position, we would never act that way, right?

Leaders have to be in control, not only of their surroundings but also of their own lives. Like the church leader discussed in today's seed, a Christian woman who is a leader (wife, mother, community volunteer, boss) must also run her life well.

We may not all be employers or supervisors, but as Christian women we are all leaders in our homes. If we haven't demonstrated

Dig Deeper:

"Self-controlled" is sometimes translated "sober" and means to be of sound mind, able to limit one's own freedom against passions and desires.

that we can run those well, we shouldn't be seeking more duties elsewhere.

A Christian woman must be watchful against the tricks of Satan, the enemy, who would seek to have her make bad decisions (1 Peter 5:8). She must be respectable so she can be an example to others. She should be hospitable and able to teach others about her faith. All of this means she is to be above reproach, so she does not give anyone a valid reason for talking badly about her and destroying her Christian witness.

Background Bulb:

When the apostle Paul departed from Ephesus, he left Timothy, a young pastor, in charge. Timothy not only had to run the church but also had to lead other church leaders, many of whom were older than he was. In today's seed Paul gives Timothy a blueprint for recognizing a person who is ready to lead.

Sprout and Scatter:

Do your church leaders cringe when they see you coming? Is your attitude and lifestyle one that encourages them? You can help your leaders rule joyfully by exhibiting the same qualities you expect them to exhibit toward you. Be respectable in your lifestyle, hospitable to other church members and visitors, be willing to teach what you know about your faith, and live a self-controlled life. Write an encouraging note to a leader today, thanking him or her for exhibiting one or more godly qualities.

Think about it:

Who do you lead?

_____

_____

What areas of your life are "above reproach"?

_____

_____

Which area from today's seed will you work to bring under control?

_____

_____

Prayer Pot:

Lord, guide me as I lead . . .

_____

_____

_____

_____

_____

_____

A good leader for Christ is a good follower of Christ.

Running Wild

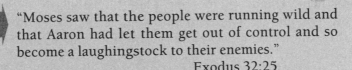

*Today's
Seed*

"Moses saw that the people were running wild and that Aaron had let them get out of control and so become a laughingstock to their enemies."

Exodus 32:25

Joe had led a wild life, and the evidence was all around him. Empty bottles and fast food wrappers littered his tables and chairs. Dirty dishes were piled in teetering stacks in the sink. Smelly layers of laundry carpeted the bathroom floor. But Joe didn't have time to clean. He was too busy dodging creditors, partying with friends, and trying to figure out what to do about his girlfriend's pregnancy.

Joe felt ashamed. He'd run wild so long that his life was completely out of control. He was a mess. A laughingstock.

Joe's situation might seem far-fetched compared to our own lives, but let's look again. Do we ever overspend, overeat, or overindulge in other damaging activities? Once we start "running wild," it's hard to slow down. The path runs downhill, *away* from self-control.

As today's seed illustrates, when we fail to exercise self-control, we inevitably make fools not only of ourselves, but also of God's reputation. While Moses was on the mountain receiving the Ten

Dig Deeper:
The Hebrew word for "laughingstock" describes someone who receives scornful whispers from hostile spectators. When we cast off restraint, we bring shame upon ourselves.

Commandments, the Israelites were down below living wildly, contrary to God's laws. They even talked Aaron into making an idol for them! The people became a laughingstock to the surrounding enemies because their wild actions led to their downfall—three thousand men were killed in punishment for their idolatry.

Our lack of self-control can make us laughingstocks to non-Christians when our actions contradict our words. Remember that uncontrolled living is self-defeating and detrimental to your witness.

Background Bulb:

When Moses arrived and questioned Aaron, he had one of the lamest excuses ever told. He said, "So I told them, 'Whoever has any gold jewelry, take it off.' Then they gave me the gold, and I threw it into the fire, and out came this calf!" (Exodus 32:24). In other words, Aaron claimed his part in the Israelites' sin was minuscule. Therefore, he couldn't really be held responsible. That excuse didn't fly with Moses, or with God. Taking part in sin makes us guilty, no matter what role we play.

Weed and Water:

Since you can't change the past, think about the future. What do you want to happen in your life, and what *don't* you want to happen? Write down these ideas, thinking only of things over which you have control. For example, you could write: "I want to have a balanced budget. I will not overspend with my credit card." "I want to be a person of integrity. I will not gossip at work."

Think about it:

In what areas are you, or might you be, running wild?

_____

_____

How could a non-Christian view your lack of self-control in a way that would reflect negatively upon God?

_____

_____

What can you do to gain control in these areas?

_____

_____

Prayer Pot:

Lord, I surrender to you my lack of self-control in the area(s) of . . .

_____

_____

_____

_____

_____

When you fail to plan, you plan to fail.

Keep in Step

Today's Seed

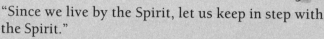

"Since we live by the Spirit, let us keep in step with the Spirit."

Galatians 5:25

A little boy walks behind his daddy in a field, putting his tiny shoe into every footprint of his father's big boot. A novice ballerina tries to follow the teacher's instructions for each dance step. A military recruit struggles to keep the formation straight with perfect steps.

Gathering spiritual fruit is a journey. Our job is to keep in step. None of us is filled with love, joy, and peace in every situation. None of us can say we are always faithful, patient, and completely in control. We all experience those times when we are not kind, gentle, or meek.

God knows that our lives are journeys. He knows that we are still in the orchard gathering fruit. He doesn't fault us for not having our basket full, but he does fault us when we stop gathering. As we have looked at the fruit of the Spirit together, it becomes clear that we cannot produce these attributes alone. Only through the power of the Holy Spirit will we blossom and form fruit.

Dig Deeper:

The phrase "keep in step" comes from the Greek word *stoicheo,* meaning to march in line like a soldier. Our captain is Jesus. Forward march!

Let's make our goal to gather the fruit, enjoy the full rich flavor of each bite, and keep gathering. The risks are high. The limb may shake and wave in the wind. We may have to climb ladders. We may have to reach and stretch. But the reward is great—delightful spiritual fruit. When we keep in step with the Spirit of God, we are blessed and we become a blessing to others.

Weed and Water:

Once we learn about the fruit of the Spirit, we want a basket full. The only way we can gather fruit is to go out on a limb—that's where the fruit is. Going out on the limb means trusting God when the evidence says there is no hope. By doing so we learn obedience—the radical and responsive kind. Gradually, we can obey when it seems illogical. Respond by doing everything God asks. Cling to the branch and go for the fruit!

Sprout and Scatter:

A tree looks most beautiful when it is covered with beautiful fruit. That's what the tree was made for. You are made to be a fruit bearer too. Let your fruit show. Put it on display in conversation, attitudes, and actions. Show the world what God has done for you by producing these attributes. Memorize the names of the nine fruits and make a mental checklist. As you go through your day, display each attribute at least once.

Think about it:

Which spiritual fruit comes most naturally for you?

_____

_____

Which spiritual fruit is most difficult to display?

_____

_____

_____

How can you better keep in step with the Spirit?

_____

_____

Prayer Pot:

Lord, help me follow you to the orchard and gather fruit
when . . .

_____

_____

_____

_____

_____

The fruit of the Spirit is like sweet
ambrosia to those who keep in step
with the Holy Spirit.

About the Contributors

Sharon Norris Elliot is a published author and popular speaker who touches the lives of her audiences at conferences, women's retreats, seminars, church, and school programs. She teaches high school English and journalism in Inglewood, California. Sharon and her husband, James, enjoy their two teenage sons. (4–33, 151–180, 238–267)

Karen Porter is an author, Bible teacher, and inspirational speaker from Texas. She is Vice President of a major food company. She has been published in a variety of national magazines including *Discipleship Journal* and has written Sunday school curriculum for Lifeway. (1–3, 34–90, 181–207, 268–270)

Denine Ziegler has served as nursery director, Sunday school teacher, and youth leader. She and her husband live in southeastern Pennsylvania. Denine's byline has appeared in the *Kutztown Patriot, Vocational Biographies,* and *Berks County Living Magazine.* (91–150, 208–237)

Scripture Index
Old Testament

Genesis
3:22 163
6:3 109
11 167
16:5 115

Exodus
16:12–25 257
32:24 266
32:25 265

Deuteronomy
15:8 256
22:20–21 17

1 Samuel
1:11 214
12:23a 193
16:7 233
18:1 25
18:7 19
23:17 26

2 Samuel
6:14 161

Nehemiah
Book of Nehemiah 52

Esther
7:3 211

Job
Book of Job 10–11
2:9 11

Psalms
4:1 86
4:7 58
4:8 85
19:8 52
23:6 159
27:13 157
34:8 151
36:7 9

57:10 184
81:13 74
89:8 185
103:10 130
105:8 181
116:5 136
116:7 40
119:33–40 149
119:37 148
122:6 75
126:6 46
133:1 166
141:3 252
145:7 160
150 161

Proverbs
11:16 139
14:29 12
14:30 21
14:30 79
15:1 223
15:23 169
16:28 237
17:17 25
25:11 171
25:16 256
25:28 259
29:23 24
31:10–31 140
31:20 140
31:31 139

Isaiah
14:12–15 23
28:17 52
30 107
30:18 106
39–40 98
40:29–31 97
43:25 130

Boldface references indicate those that appear at the beginning of a study-devotional. All other references appear within the lesson texts.

48:18 74
53 232

Jeremiah
15:16 53

Lamentations
3:22–23 89
3:25–26 112

Ezekiel
28:11–19 23

Daniel
1:8 238

Jonah
2:8 196

Micah
6:8 121
7:1 68
7:7 67
7:18b 68

New Testament

Matthew
1:19 17
5–7 155
5:5 232
5:9 82
6:9–13 194
7:11 154
17 8
19:13 194
19:13–15 209
19:14 208
19:16–24 248
20:16 134
23:33 235
25:34–40 5
26:42 182

Mark
6:31 41
10:13–16 209
14 8

Luke
6:28 194
6:31 134
10:33–34 124
15:11–32 7
18:15–17 209
19:41–42 73

John
4:4–30 145
8:4–11 16
8:5 16
8:7 16
10:14–15 220

13:15 5
14:6 142
14:23 13
14:27 70
16:20b 44
17:20–21 194
20:24–25 152
21:20 8

Acts
2–3 203
8:8 49
11:18 37
16:25 43

Romans
1:7–8 179
3:23 53
5:1 53
5:8 ....4, 53
6:23 53
10:9–10 53
10:13 53
12:1 30
12:10 205
12:18 88
13:14 241
15:14 178

1 Corinthians
6:18–20 253
13:4a 10
13:4b 16
13:4c 19
13:4d 22

2 Corinthians
1:22 80
3:2 188
3:4–5 187–188
5:14–15 28
12:7–8 100
12:10 101

Galatians
5:1 2
5:17 242
5:22–23 1
5:25 268
6:10 145

Ephesians
2:8–9 142
2:14 71
3:17 80
4:2 103
5:19 61

Philippians
3 187
4:5 226
4:5–7 80
4:11 76
4:12–13 76

Colossians
3:12 95
3:12, 14 94
3:13 89
3:15 81

1 Thessalonians
2:6b–7 229
2:8–9 229–230

Books of Timothy 176

1 Timothy
3:2 262
3:7 175
6:9 247

4:16 202

2 Timothy
3:1–3 133

Titus
3:2 235

Philemon
1:7 34

James
1:7 23
1:12 118
1:14 244
1:19–20 224
1:26 251
2:17 143
3:5–9 251
5:7–8 91
5:12 182

1 Peter
3:1–6 65
3:4 64
3:10 250
3:15b–16 217
5:7 193
5:8 263

2 Peter
1:4–5 ....172, 178

1 John
1:5 200
1:7 200
1:9 199
3:1 7
4:18 31

3 John
1:4 55
1:5 127

Revelation
5:8–9 62
14:12 118

Subject and Name Index

A

Aaron, 265–266
Abraham (Abram), 115–116, 181, 248
Abundance, 76–77, 247–249
Acceptance of others, 89, 103–105, 203
Accountability, 116, 260
Acquaintances, 25–26
Actions, 5, 34–36, 125, 203
Adam and Eve, 163–164, 185, 224
Adulterous woman, 16–17
Adversity (*see* Troubles)
Advice, 121, 137, 143, 170
Aesop, 18
Affection, 25–26, 136
Angels, 17, 22–23, 71, 182
Anger, 80, 88–90, 95, 103–105,
    190–191, 199, 223–225
Annoyance, 65, 103–105, 131
Anxiety, 65, 71, 80, 85–87, 193
Apology, 104
Arabs, 116
Arrogance (*see* Pride)

B

Babel, tower of, 167
Babylon, 98, 121, 239
Barna (George) Research, 203
Baxter, Richard, 168
Beauty, 64–66
Beliefs, Christian, 202–204
Betrayal, 163
the Bible, 52–54, 148–149, 164, 178,
    202, 206, 242
Blessings, 23, 59, 71, 106–108, 158–159,
    185
Boredom, 35
Borland, Hal, 93
Born again (*see* Salvation)
Bruce and Stan, 183
Burnout, 97–99
Busch, Wilhelm, 156

C

Calm (*see* Peace)
Caring for others, 47, 136–138

Carlyle, Thomas, 180
Carney, Julia A. Fletcher, 138
Celebration, 43, 47, 50, 61–63, 160–162
Chambers, Oswald, 42
Chaos, 2, 65, 80
Charity, 139–140, 168
Cheerfulness (*see* Joy)
Childbirth, 44, 55
Children, 13–14, 32, 55–57, 125,
    154–156, 194, 208–210, 221, 251
Choices, 56, 164
Christian community/fellowship,
    103–105, 118–119, 127–128,
    166–168, 175–177, 200, 202–204,
    205–207, 245
Christianity (doctrine), 202–204
Christian life, 94–95, 199–201,
    229–231, 241–243, 262–264,
    265–267
Christian witness, 32, 37–39, 50, 55–57,
    65, 71, 74, 77, 82, 92, 110, 119, 122,
    145–146, 175–176, 179, 209, 212,
    217–219, 229–231, 262–264,
    265–267, 269
the Church (*see* Christian
    community/fellowship)
Closeness, 13–15
Comfort, 136–137
Communication, 13–15, 14, 169–171,
    235–237, 250–252
Companionship, 25–26
Compassion, 2, 16–17, 94, 124–126,
    136–138, 206
Complaining, 59, 83, 88–90, 112–113
Conceit (*see* Pride)
Confidence, 187–189
Conflict, 73, 88–90, 103–104, 166–168
Conscience, 80, 163
Contentment, 76–78
Conversation (*see* Words)
Cooperation, 82–83, 166–168
Courage, 80
Coveting (*see* Envy)
Cravings, 241–243, 244–246

Creation, 184–186
Criticism, 26, 88–90
the Cross, 1, 4, 29, 131, 155, 182
Crying (see Weeping)

D

Dancing, 61–62, 161
Daniel, 238–239
David (King), 19–20, 25–26, 62, 86,
    157, 161
Death, 31, 163–164
Deborah, 140
Decisions, 56, 164
Demons, 43
Desires, 241–243, 244–246
Despair, 67–68
Difficulties (see Troubles)
Difficult people, 10–12, 16–18, 65,
    88–90, 103–105, 124–126,
    205–207, 223–225, 226–228
Diplomacy, 82–84
Disappointment, 2, 158, 190–191
Discernment, 164
Discord (see Conflict)
"Divine appointment," 146
Doctrine, Christian, 202–204
Doubt, 112–113

E

Eden, Garden of (see Adam and Eve)
Eli (high priest), 214–215
Embarrassment, 118–120
Empathy, 10–12, 11
Encouragement, 26, 35, 169–171
Endurance (see Patience)
Enemies, 16–18, 73–74, 86, 194,
    223–225, 226–227, 235–237
Engedi (mountains), 86
Envy, 2, 19–21, 79–81, 89
Esther (Queen), 211–212
Eternal life, 31, 74, 101, 118–119
Eve, Adam and, 163–164, 185, 224
Evil, 163–165, 244
Evil spirits, 43
Example, setting, 55–56
Excuses, 177
Experience, 178–180
Ezra, 52

F

Fairness, 163
Faith, 11, 91–92, 118–119, 142–144,
    152, 157, 172–173, 202–204, 208
    Faithfulness, 1–2, 26, 181–207
    confidence, 187–189
    creation as teaching, 184–186
    doctrine, 202–204
    to each other, 205–207
    of Jesus, 190–192
    possessions and, 196–198
    in prayer, 193–195
    promises, 181–183
    walking in, 199–201
Fake, being (see Hypocrisy)
Family, 13–15, 103, 166–167,
    226–227, 235–237
Father, God as, 7–8, 154–156
Fatherhood, 7–8, 154–156
Fatigue, 97–99
Faults, 88–90
Fear, 31–33, 80, 85–87
Food, 256–258
Forbearance, 103–104
Forgiveness of sin, 28, 82, 88–90, 95,
    116, 122, 130–132, 200
Forgiving others, 83, 88–90, 95,
    130–132
Franklin, Benjamin, 177
Freedom, 2
Friendship, 25–27, 128, 137, 140,
    195, 200
Fruit of the Spirit, 1–3, 268–270

G

Gaius, 55–56, 127–128
Galilee, Sea of, 71
Gamaliel, 77
Garden of Eden (see Adam and Eve)
Garden of Gethsemane, 8, 182
Generosity (see Giving)
Gentiles, 37–38
Gentleness, 1–2, 64–66, 94, 103,
    208–237
    anger, as soothing, 223–225
    with children, 208–210
    in communication, 235–237

the good shepherd, 220–222
greatness as, 211–213
"horizontal," 226–228
as love in action, 229–231
and meekness, 232–234
surrender to God, 214–216
in witnessing, 217–219
George Barna Research, 203
Gethsemane, Garden of, 8, 182
Gifts from God, 23, 154–156
Giving, 2, 7, 70, 124–125
Godliness, 122
God's Word (*see* Bible)
Goliath, 19
Good deeds, 142–144
Goodness, 1–2, 139, 151–180
    cultivation of, 172–174
    vs. evil, 163–165
    experience in, 178–180
    of God, 151–153
    good gifts, 154–156
    in hard times, 157–159
    praising God's, 160–162
    reputation, 175–177
    unity, 166–168
    words, timely, 169–171
Good Samaritan, the, 125
Gossip, 163, 235–237, 250–252
Grace (God's), 31, 71, 130–132,
    142–144, 196–197, 220–221
Grace (of character), 157–158
Graciousness, 139–140
Gratitude, 29, 80
Greatness, 211–213
Greed, 77, 247–249
Grief, 80, 163, 190–191. (*See also*
    Suffering; Troubles)
Grievances, 88–90, 95
Growth, spiritual, 37–38, 55–56, 94–95,
    113, 172–173, 220, 268–270
Grudges, 88–90
Grumbling (*see* Complaining)
Guidance, God's, 158
Guilt, 80

H

Habits, 172–173, 241–243, 244–246
Hagar, 115–116

Hamilton, Jane, 174
Hannah, 214–215
Happiness (*see* Joy)
Hardship (*see* Troubles)
Harmony (*see* Unity)
Harsh behavior, 2, 226–228
Hatred, 80
Healing, 49, 100–102, 137
Heart, 79–81
Heaven (*see* Eternal life)
Help, asking for, 67
Helping others (*see* Service)
Hemingway, Ernest, 255
Holidays, 58–60
Holiness, 173
Holy Spirit, 1–2, 8, 71–72, 80, 89, 92,
    94, 134, 164, 268
Honesty, 182, 236, 259–260
Hope, 50, 97–99, 101, 118–119, 189,
    218
Horace, 240
Hospitality, 125, 127–129, 263
Hugo, Victor, 87
Human nature, 70–71, 80, 134
Humiliation, 67, 118–120
Humility, 2, 22–24, 94, 103, 122,
    235–236
Husbands, 65
Hymns (*see* Singing)
Hypocrisy, 226–227, 235–237

I

Illness, 100–101, 191
Impatience (*see* Patience)
Inadequacy, feelings of, 8
Infidelity, 2, 14
Injustice, 163
Insomnia, 85–87
Integrity, 94, 182
Intimacy, 13–15, 25–26
Irritation (*see* Annoyance)
Isaac, 116, 181
Ishmael, 115–116
Israel, 73–75, 98, 107, 121–122, 181,
    185, 194

J

Jacob, 181

Jealousy (*see* Envy)
Jerusalem, 50, 73–75, 98
Jewish Christians, 37–38, 49–50
Job (person), 10–11, 248
John, 8, 55–56, 128
Johnstone, Patrick, 203
John the Baptist, 217
Jonah, 196–197
Jonathan, 25–26
Joseph (father of Jesus), 17
Joy, 1–2, 13, 34–63, 68, 80, 169–170
    action, as taking, 34–36
    in the Bible, 52–54
    delights, unexpected, 58–60
    parental, 55–57
    resting, as found in, 40–42
    trouble, in time of, 43–45
    as uniting force, 49–51
    weeping turned to, 46–48
    in witnessing, 37–39
    in worship, 61–63
Judah (place), 121–122
Judging others, 17, 137, 151, 245
Judgment, God's, 110
Justice, 52–53, 163

K

Kindness, 1–2, 16–18, 94, 121–150, 170
    the art, 121–123
    and compassion, 136–138
    God's bounty of, 148–150
    and God's grace, 142–143
    hospitality, 127–129
    intentional, 145–147
    a kindhearted woman, 139–141
    mercy, 130–132
    neighborly, 124–126
    vs. selfishness, 133–135
King's Manifesto, 155
Knowledge, 172, 178–180

L

Law of Moses, 52, 239
Lazarus, 190–191
Leadership, 175–177, 211–213, 262–264
Leading, God's, 113, 164, 221, 239

"Letting God," 67–69
Liberty, 168
Light, 199–200
Listening to others, 47, 137
Love, 1–2, 4–33, 80, 94, 103, 127, 129, 136, 157–158, 167
    envy, as suppressing, 19–21
    fear and, 31–33
    in friendship, 25–27
    and giving, 7–9
    and intimacy, 13–15
    kindness and, 16–18
    patience and, 10–12
    pride, as not, 22–24
    service, as through, 28–30
    showing, 4–6, 14
    unconditional, 7–9, 14
Lucifer, 22–23
Lust, 253–255
Luther, Martin, 109
Lying, 236, 259–260

M

Marriage, 64–66, 139–140, 158, 236
Martha, 190–191
Martin, Civilla D., 186
Mary (mother of Jesus), 8, 17
Mary (sister of Martha), 190–191
Maturity, 37, 178–180
Meditation (*see* Prayer)
Meekness, 232–234
Mercy of God, 28–29, 68, 82
Mercy toward others, 17, 121–122, 130–132
Micah, 67–68, 121–122
Michal, 161
Ministry (*see* Christian witness)
Miriam, 61
Misunderstandings, 88–90
Modesty, 94
Molière, 258
Money (*see* Wealth)
Moses, 181, 265–266
Moses, law of, 52
Motherhood, 139–140, 221
Mount of Olives, 73
Music, 61–62, 161

N

Nature, 164
Nineveh, 196–197
Noah, 109–110, 181
Nonbelievers (*see* Unbelievers)

O

Obeying God, 13–14, 53, 119, 173,
    220–221, 239, 269
Olives, Mount of, 73
Onesimus, 35
Optimism, 158
Overeating, 256–258

P

Pain (*see* Suffering; Troubles)
Parenthood, 32, 55–57, 154–156
Patience, 1–2, 10–12, 65, 91–120
    in affliction, 100–102
    with Christians, 103–105
    developing, 94–96
    end of God's, 109–111
    endurance, 118–120
    of God, 106–108
    with God, 112–114
    impatience, consequences of, 115–117
    in practice, 91–93
    and renewal, 97–99
Paul, 1–2, 34–35, 43–44, 76–77, 94–95,
    100–101, 134, 176, 178–179,
    187–188, 202, 203, 205, 226–227,
    262–263
Peace, 1–2, 64–90, 166
    beauty and, 64–66
    contentment, 76–78
    forgiveness as bringing, 88–90
    of God, 70–72
    of heart, 79–81
    for Jerusalem, 73–75
    of "letting God," 67–69
    peacemakers, 82–84
    in sleep, 85–87
Peacemakers, 82–84
Peninnah, 214–215
Pentecost, 8
Persecution, 49–50, 50, 118–120
Perseverance, 91–92, 202

Persia, 211–212
Pessimism, 59
Peter, 185, 202, 217–218
Pharisees, 83, 217, 235
Philemon, 34–35
Philip, 49–50
Planning, 266–267
Possessions, 76–78, 196–198, 247–249
Poverty, 76–78, 80
Power, 229–230
Power of God, 67, 97–98, 97–99, 101,
    118
Practice, 172–173
Praising God (*see* Worship)
Prayer, 2, 14, 27–28, 35, 41, 67–69, 80,
    86, 92, 98, 112–114, 125, 157–158,
    161, 164, 185, 193–195, 206–207,
    233
Pride, 22–24, 67, 133
Problems (*see* Troubles)
Procrastination, 259–260
Prodigal son, 7–8
Promised Land, 61–62
Promises, 181–183
Purity, 94, 253–255

Q

Quietness, 40–42, 64–66, 112–114

R

Reconciliation, 82–84, 83, 88–90, 95
Rejection, 118–119
Rejoicing (*see* Celebration)
Relaxation (*see* Rest)
Reliability (*see* Faithfulness)
Religion, 202–204
Renewal, 97–99
Reputation, 175–177, 179, 182,
    262–263
Resentment, 88–90. (*See also* Anger)
Resolve, 238–240
Respect, 139–141, 172, 218
Rest, 40–42, 58–59
Resurrection of Jesus, 1, 5, 8
Revenge, 88–90
Reverence, 31
Riches (*see* Wealth)

Righteousness, 52–53, 83, 157–158
Rockefeller, John D., 223
Rusthoi, Esther Kerr, 120
Ruth, 212

S

Sabbath, 40–42
Sacrifice of Jesus (*see* Cross)
Sadness (*see* Grief; Suffering)
Safety, 85–87
Salvation, 1–2, 31, 37–38, 53, 55, 80,
   83, 110–111, 142–144, 173
Samaria, 49–50
Samaritan, the Good, 124–125
Samaritan woman, 145
Samuel, 194, 214–215
Sarah (Sarai), 115–116
Satan, 22–23, 224
Satisfaction, 58, 76–77
Saul (King), 19–20, 25–26, 86, 194
Sayers, Dorothy L., 153
Scam artists, 125
Scripture (*see* Bible)
Sea of Galilee, 71
the Second Coming, 74, 110, 119,
   134, 181
Secrets, 195, 199–201
Security, 13–15, 64–65
Self-centeredness, 47
Self-control, 1–2, 214, 236
   and desires, 241–243
   with food, 256–258
   lack of, 259–261, 265–267
   leadership, 262–264
   resolve, 238–240
   sexual sin, 253–255
   in speech, 250–252
   temptation, 244–246
   wants vs. needs, 247–249
Self-discipline, 37
Self-doubt, 8
Selfishness, 2, 35, 80, 133–135, 254
Self-respect, 23
Sermon on the Mount, 155
Service, 5, 28–30, 29, 34–36, 71, 83,
   139–140, 145–147, 173, 229–231
Sex, 2, 14
Sexual sin, 253–255

Shalom, 70
Shepherd, 220–222
Sickness, 100–101, 191
Silas, 43–44, 229–230
Sin, 4–5, 70–71, 80, 82, 89, 130–132,
   163–165, 199–201, 244–246,
   253–255, 266
Sincerity, 83, 130, 137, 226–227
Singing, 43–44, 61–62
Slander (*see* Gossip)
Slave girl, the, 43
Sleep, 85–87
Solomon, 248
Sorrow (*see* Grief; Suffering)
Speech (*see* Words)
Spirit (*see* Holy Spirit)
Spiritual growth, 37–38, 55–56,
   94–95, 113, 172–173, 220,
   268–270
Spurgeon, Charles H., 165
Stephen, 50
Strength, 76–77, 97–99, 100–101,
   232–234
Submissiveness, 65
Success, 23, 187–189, 196–198
Suffering, 46–48, 100–102. (*See also*
   Troubles)
Sunday, 40–42
Supportiveness, 25–27, 35, 47,
   169–171, 173, 205–207
Surprises, 58–60
Surrender to God, 214–216
Sympathy, 124–125

T

Tact, 82–84
Talent (*see* Gifts from God)
Tears (*see* Weeping)
Temper (*see* Anger)
Temptation, 175–177, 244–246
ten Boom, Corrie, 157
Thankfulness, 29, 80
Thomas, 152
Thoreau, Henry David, 33
Thoughtfulness, 172
Timothy, 134, 176, 203, 229–230,
   262–263
Tolerance (*see* Acceptance of others)

Tower of Babel, 167
Tranquillity (*see* Peace)
the Transfiguration, 8
Trauma (*see* Suffering)
Trials (*see* Troubles)
Trinity, 1
Troubles, 5, 11, 43–45, 46–48, 49–50,
    70–71, 85–86, 100–102, 118–120,
    157–159, 193–195
Trusting God, 32, 67–69, 91–92, 107,
    118–119, 142–143, 155, 215
Trustworthiness, 25–26, 208
Truth, 55, 202–204

U

Unbelievers, 109–110, 118–120, 122
Unconditional love, 7–8, 7–9, 14
Understanding others, 10–12
Unfairness, 163
Unity, 166–168
Usefulness, 16, 34–36, 139–140

V

Vacation, 58–60. (*See also* Rest)
Values, 122, 149, 182, 196–198, 241
Vashti (Queen), 211–212
Virtues, 94–96, 129, 172–173

W

Waiting on God, 67–69, 97–99,
    106–108, 112–114
War, 73–74, 82–84
Weakness, 232–233
Weaknesses (physical), 100–101
Wealth, 2, 32, 59, 76–77, 133, 149,
    196–198, 247–249
Weeping, 46–48, 73–74
Wickedness (*see* Evil)
Wilson, Flip, 244
Wisdom, 83, 178–180
Witnessing (*see* Christian witness)
Wives, 65, 139–140
Womanhood, 64–66, 139–141, 164,
    250, 254, 262–263
Word of God (*see* Bible)
Words, 169–171, 223–225, 235–237,
    250–252
Work (labor), 58, 164
Works (deeds), 142–143
Worry, 31–33, 80, 85–87
Worship, 29, 61–63, 160–162, 185
Wrath (*see* Anger)

X

Xerxes (King), 211–212